Guitar Chords

FOR

DUMMIES®

By Antoine Polin

⊛ WILEY

A John Wiley and Sons, Ltd, Publication

Guitar Chords For Dummies®

Published by
John Wiley & Sons, Ltd
The Atrium
Southern Gate
Chichester
West Sussex
PO19 8SQ
England

Email (for orders and customer service enquires): cs-books@wiley.co.uk

Visit our Home Page on www.wiley.com

©Éditions First, 2008. Publié en accord avec Wiley Publishing, Inc.

Translation copyright © 2010 John Wiley & Sons, Ltd, Chichester, West Sussex, England

Published by John Wiley & Sons, Ltd, Chichester, West Sussex

First published by Éditions First, 2008

For general information on our other products and services, please contact our Customer Care Department within the US at 877-762-2974, outside the US at 317-572-3993, or fax 317-572-4002.

For technical support, please visit www.wiley.com/techsupport.

Wiley also publishes its books in a variety of electronic formats. Some content that appears in print may not be available in electronic books.

British Library Cataloguing in Publication Data: A catalogue record for this book is available from the British Library

ISBN: 978-0-470-66603-6

Printed and bound in Great Britain by Bell & Bain Ltd., Glasgow

10 9 8 7 6 5

WILEY

About the Author

Antoine Polin studied music at Berklee College of Music in Boston from which he emerged as a *cum laude* graduate. Performing regularly as a professional guitarist he won the 'Young Paris Talent' prize in 2004 for the recording of his second album.

The holder of the French State Diploma in jazz, he also teaches the guitar and conducts musical ensembles on both amateur and professional training courses at the School of Jazz in Tours.

Publisher's Acknowledgments

We're proud of this book; please send us your comments through our Dummies online registration form located at www.dummies.com/register/.

Some of the people who helped bring this book to market include the following:

Acquisitions, Editorial and Media Development

Project Editor: Rachael Chilvers

Content Editor: Jo Theedom

Assistant Editor: Ben Kemble

Commissioning Editor: David Palmer

Production Manager: Daniel Mersey

Cover Photos: © Carsten Reisinger/ Alamy

Composition Services

Project Coordinator: Lynsey Stanford

Layout and Graphics: Joyce Haughey, Rashell Smith, Erin Zeltner

Proofreader: Laura Albert

Indexer: Ty Koontz

Contents at a Glance

Table of Contents

Part II: D$^{\flat}$/ C$^{\sharp}$-family Chords 53

Part IV: E♭/D#-family Chords 113

Part V: E-family Chords *139*

Part VIII: G-family Chords 219

Part IX: A♭/G♯ Chords 247

Part XII: B-family Chords 325

Introduction

· ·

*T*he guitar has become an iconic instrument since the beginning of the 20th century. It is often associated with the blues, rock and pop styles of music. Who can forget those images of Jimi Hendrix making his electric guitar wail and other guitar greats such as Jimmy Page (Led Zeppelin), Brian May (Queen) and Eric Clapton? The list is a long one! Nevertheless, this instrument can likewise be found in many other types of music: classical, flamenco, Brazilian, country, metal, jazz, African, folk . . . . it is almost impossible to list them all, such is the worldwide popularity of the guitar.

Often regarded as a solo instrument, in the majority of cases, the guitar is used as an accompaniment, given its harmonic possibilities (since it allows you to play chords, unlike a saxophone or trumpet, for example, which can only play one note at a time). It is precisely this characteristic which we address in this book.

Foolish Assumptions

For a guitarist, learning to play chords is essential in order to be able to play the instrument, at any level. In creating this book, I assume that:

> ✔ You're a beginner, you have some scores or chord progressions of your favourite pieces, but you don't understand the chord symbols or don't know where to play them on your guitar.

✔ You're a non-beginner wanting to practice more complex sounds, but are having difficulty in locating the neck position of the notes which give chords such special colours.

✔ You're a beginner or non-beginner, but above all interested in getting to know the guitar and its harmonic possibilities better, discovering new sounds for composing, arranging or adapting existing pieces, and, most of all, enjoying yourself.

About This Book

In this book we explore thirty types of chords in each key. The various chords are organised in a logical way, to enable you to find the information you're looking for easily.

In the case of most chords, a short explanation enables you to understand how to move from one chord to another; for example, how to move from D major to D minor, the change involving the notes and the positioning of the fingers.

You can use this book in two different ways:

✔ **As a dictionary.** You can search for just one or more chords in a specific key in order to play a piece: in which case you can consult the index at the back of the book in order to identify the relevant chord. The photos and diagrams help you to position your fingers on the neck in order to achieve the desired result.

✔ **As a method.** We tried to make this book a good teaching aid. As stated earlier, short explanations of the chords are provided so that you can understand how they're constructed.

You can pick any given chord (say, D), begin with the simplest form of the chord (D major) and then progress steadily through the book, listening to and visualizing each change in order to arrive at the most 'complex' sounds (such as $D^{7\flat13}$). You can then understand how chords are constructed so that, ultimately, you'll be able to find and create the ones you need for yourself.

With this approach in mind, the rest of this section explains the step-by-step logic behind the construction of chords as well as the arrangement of notes on the neck of the guitar.

Family names

Each chord **family name** denotes its root (for example, Do, expressed as *C*) and its quality (such as *min7*).

Alternative notations of the chord can be found to the right of this name, in brackets. For example, there are several different ways of writing a minor 7th chord: min7, m7 and -7 are three possibilities.

Under the family name you will find a line listing the notes of the chord according to their function (Root = Do (C); maj 3rd = E; and so on).

What does the asterisk mean?

You can sometimes find a little **asterisk (*)** after the name of the chord in the family name. It merely indicates that the chord in question is a basic one, with which you should familiarise yourself to ensure that you start off on the right foot.

Diagrams

A chord **diagram** graphically conveys the section of the neck on which the chord is placed. In a diagram, each note fretted is represented by a dot within which the function of the note in the chord is specified (root, third, fifth, seventh and so on).

The **X**s and **O**s situated at the top of the neck show you if the string beside which the symbol appears should be played ('open') or not.

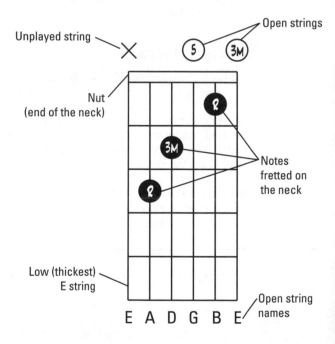

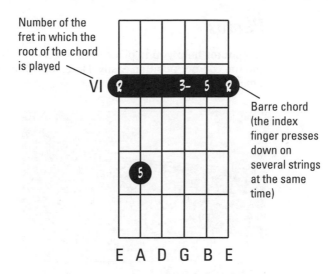

Number of the fret in which the root of the chord is played

Barre chord (the index finger presses down on several strings at the same time)

E A D G B E

In a diagram, each dot indicates the note to be played as well as the function of that note in the chord:

R	: Root	**Dim7**	: Diminished seventh
3 -	: Minor third	**7 -**	: Minor seventh
M3	: Major third	**M7**	: Major seventh
4	: Perfect fourth	**9**♭	: Minor ninth
4♯	: Augmented fourth	**9**	: Major ninth
5♭	: Diminished fifth	**9**♯	: Augmented ninth
5	: Perfect fifth	**11**	: Perfect eleventh
5♯	: Augmented fifth	**11**♯	: Augmented eleventh
6 -	: Minor sixth	**13**	: Major thirteenth
M6	: Major sixth	**13**♭	: Minor thirteenth

Photos

The **photos** help you to place your fingers so you can find the correct position easily. Here, for example, is the E major chord:

Icons

The **icons** indicate useful and important items of information throughout the book to make for easy reading.

This icon shows you the important information to remember.

You may sometimes find certain chords difficult to play! This icon highlights a trick for simplifying the fingering of chords so that you'll always be able to play them.

A Little Theory . . .

Theory is often given a bad press and frightens a large number of amateur (and professional!) musicians. Nevertheless, it's very useful for understanding music as well as your instrument. Never forget that **theory serves music**, not the other way round!

This section addresses some very simple principles concerning chord construction.

The skeleton

We refer to all the notes which give a chord its basic sound as the 'skeleton'.

The skeleton of a basic chord generally consists of three notes:

- ✔ The **root**, which gives its name to the chord (for example, in the case of a C major chord, the root is C)
- ✔ The **third**, which gives the chord a major or minor tone
- ✔ The **fifth**

This skeleton may include a sixth or seventh, which would give the chord a slightly 'richer' texture. (Remember: a richer or more complex chord tone doesn't necessarily mean a more beautiful tone/sound, it is all a question of taste and context!)

Any chord you may wish to play is taken from a *scale*, that is, a series of (in general) seven notes, which have a particular combined sound (often called *colour*).

Take a look at what to do in order to find a chord on the basis of a scale. For example, take the familiar scale of C major which is easy to understand since it comprises the seven natural notes (without sharps or flats) of Western-style music.

From this you take the skeleton of a C chord:

> *C major scale*: **C D E F G A B C**

Play the scale starting from the root of your chord (in this case the note C for the C chord) and give each note a number:

> 1 = C; 2 = D; 3 = E; 4 = F; 5 = G; 6 = A; 7 = B

In order to find this *C* chord, you see that a **root**, a **third** and a **fifth** are required. In this example, you can also try to find a seventh, in order to obtain a 4-tone skeleton (4 different notes).

By definition:

- ✔ The *root* is the first note of the chord and is expressed as 1
- ✔ The *third* is expressed as 3
- ✔ The *fifth* is expressed as 5
- ✔ The *seventh* is expressed as 7

You can then find:

- ✔ Root = 1 = C
- ✔ Third = 3 = E

> ✔ Fifth = 5 = G
>
> ✔ Seventh = 7 = B

The skeleton of the required C chord is thus made up of the notes C, E, G, B.

Follow the same logic in order to find an F chord. Play and count in the same way, starting from the first note of your chord (in this case the note F for the F chord):

> 1 = F; 2 = G 3 = A; 4 = B, and so on.

You should then find the following for the F chord:

> **F** (Root), **A** (Third), **C** (Fifth), **E** (Seventh)

Embellishments

You can add certain notes to chords in order to add a specific sound, or to embellish them without, however, modifying their skeleton. Such notes are referred to as *embellishments*.

In Western music, there are seven different notes (*C, D, E, F, G, A, B*) each of which may be augmented by a sharp (♯) or diminished by a flat (♭). The notes of the chord skeleton are comprised between 1 (root) and 7 (seventh). Since these embellishments would be super-imposed on the skeleton, these notes would then have names (or numbers above 7). The logic for finding them is the same as in the case of the skeleton notes. All you have to do is play the scale on the first (root) note of the chord and count starting from '8' (instead of '1' for the skeleton notes).

Take the example of the *C* chord for which you found the skeleton earlier (*C, E, G, B*) and try to find what embellishments are possible:

> **8 = C** (Skeleton root); **9 = D** (Ninth, first possible embellishment); **10 = E** (Skeleton third); **11 = F** (Eleventh, second possible embellishment); **12 = G** (Skeleton fifth); **13 = A** (Thirteenth, third possible embellishment); **14 = B** (Skeleton seventh).

As you can see, the 8th, 10th, 12th and 14th are notes already included in the skeleton. To play them again or rename them wouldn't produce any great change to the tone of the chord. It follows, therefore, that there are three types of possible embellishments: the 9th, 11th and 13th. In the case of the *C* chord, the embellishments are **D, F, A**.

Lastly, a *C* chord comprising all possible embellishments would give:

1	*3*	*5*	*7*	*9*	*11*	*13*
C	**E**	**G**	**B**	**D**	**F**	**A**

Try to find the possible embellishments for the *F* chord for yourself. You have already found its skeleton: Root = F' 3rd = A; 5th = C; 7th = E.

Follow the same procedure as with the *F* chord in order to find the embellishments:

> **8 = F** (Root of the skeleton); **9 = G** (Ninth, first possible potential); **10 = A**, and so on.

So you've found that the embellishments possible on the *F* chord are the **9th (G)**, the **11th (B)** and the **13th (D)**.

Final stage: Intervals

You've seen how to find the notes of the chord skeleton and its embellishments. There remains only one point to clear up: how do you decide if a third is major or minor? If a fifth is perfect or augmented? If a ninth is major or minor? This is where the concept of an **interval** comes in.

An *interval* is the distance separating two notes. The unit of measurement of an interval is the tone or semitone.

The distances between notes are fixed and determined as follows:

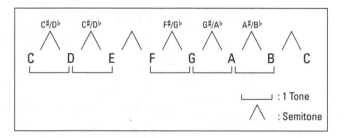

Remember that a sharp (♯) raises the note by a semitone (1 fret) and that a flat (♭) lowers it by a semitone (1 fret).

The distance between *E* and *F* and between *B* and *C* is a semitone. (Look at a piano keyboard: there's no black key (either sharp or flat) between *E* and *F* or *B* and *C*!)

Once you've reached the end of the scale, you get back to *C*. You could then begin the scale all over again, and again and again. That is what is known as an octave:

An **octave** is the same note played higher or lower. In the figure, the end *C* is the *octave above* (higher) the first *C*.

We strongly recommend that you learn the previous figure of the tones and semitones by heart; it will prove immensely valuable throughout your apprenticeship!

Now that this concept of interval has been explained, all that remains is to determine if a third is major or minor, a fifth is perfect or augmented, an eleventh is perfect or augmented, an eleventh is perfect or augmented. It's quite straightforward as there are precise rules whereby names can be given to these distances (intervals):

Bottom note	*Top note*	*Distance*
Root	Minor second (min 9th)	½ Tone
	Major second (maj 9th)	1 Tone
	Augmented second (aug 9th)	1½ Tones
Root	Minor third	1½ Tones
	Major third	3 Tones
Root	Perfect fourth (perfect 11th)	2½ Tones
	Augmented fourth (aug 11th)	3 Tones
Root	Diminished fifth	3 Tones
	Perfect fifth	3½ Tones
	Augmented fifth	4 Tones
Root	Minor sixth (min 13th)	4 Tones
	Major sixth (maj 13th)	4½ Tones
Root	Diminished seventh	4½ Tones
	Minor seventh	5 Tones
	Major seventh	5½ Tones
Root	Octave (Higher Root)	6 Tones

Two points in this table may surprise you:

✏ The augmented second and the minor third are equidistant from the root: 1½ tones. This isn't a mistake. It corresponds to more complex harmonic rules which we won't discuss here. To be sure of not mixing them up, remember that the third is the 3rd note when counting along the scale starting from the chord root note and that the second is the 2nd note. (The same logic applies in the case of the augmented fourth/diminished fifth, the augmented fifth/minor sixth and the major sixth/diminished seventh which are, respectively, equidistant from the root.)

✏ In the table and for ease of reference, the seconds are situated the same distance away from the root as the 9ths. The same applies in the case of the fourths and 11ths as well as the sixths and 13ths. They're effectively the same notes, but the 9ths, 11ths and 13ths are situated one **octave above** the seconds, fourths and sixths. We've adopted this simplified concept to help you when calculating the distances. In effect, it's altogether simpler to think that a minor 9th, for example, is ½ tone away from the root as opposed to 6 ½ tones!

With the help of the figure and the table, it becomes easy to find the name of the intervals separating two notes.

Look again at our example of the *C* chord, the skeleton of which is as follows:

Root = **C**; 3rd = **E**; 5th = **G**; 7th = **B**

Take Figure A and do the maths. You'll find:

✏ Between *C* (root) and *E*: 2 tones, so, according to the table, a major third.

✏ Between *C* and *G*: 3½ tones, so a perfect fifth.

✏ Between *C* and *B*: 5½ tones, so a major seventh.

The skeleton of the *C* chord which you'd found is therefore given the name:

C major/major seventh

The fifth isn't mentioned when it is perfect.

As regards embellishments, in the case of this chord you'd already found:

9th = **D**; 11th = **F**; 13th = **A**

Once again, by combining the use of Figure A and the table, you can see:

- Between *C* and *D* = 1 tone, so a major ninth.

- Between *C* and *F* = 2½ tones, so a major eleventh.

- Between *C* and *A* = 4½ tones, so a major thirteenth.

The embellishments of the *C* chord found are, therefore, 9th, 11th and 13th.

(No mention is made of the fact that an embellishment is major or perfect: if nothing is indicated, it is so – major or perfect – by default.)

As well as to analyse the notes of an established chord, you could also use this system to find those of a chord for yourself.

Imagine that you were trying to find the notes of a D major chord with a minor seventh and a major ninth (expressed as $D^{7\,9}$).

This chord would comprise:

- ✔ A **root** (*D*)

- ✔ A major **third**. So you start from the root and count 2 tones to find the major 3ʳᵈ, that is, *F♯*

- ✔ A perfect **fifth**: you count 3½ tones starting from the root and find: *A*

- ✔ A minor **seventh**: you count 5 tones from the root and find: *C*

- ✔ A major **ninth**: you count one tone from the root and find: *E*

The D⁷ ⁹ chord therefore consists of the notes *D, F♯, A, C and E.*

To provide you with some form of visual reference, here is a guitar neck on which the notes are marked. With the guitar, in any given chord, there is a semitone between one fret and the next, anywhere along the neck.

For the sake of clarity, this figure only shows the notes referred to as 'natural', that is, those which don't carry a sharp or flat. Remember that if you want to find a note which carries a sharp, you must augment the note by a semitone (1 fret). To find a flat note, you must diminish it by a semitone (1 fret).

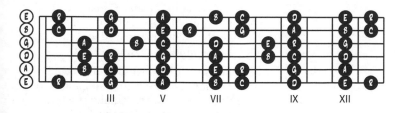

Chord Notation

In order to identify chords easily and write them down, you'll see a number of conventions and symbols throughout this book.

Chord roots are ususaly expressed as:

A = La; B = Si; C = Do; D = Re; E = Mi; F = Fa; G = Sol

You need to know this sequence by heart. It is very easy to remember and, with experience, you will notice that it appears everywhere.

Before moving on to full chord notation, here are a few essential rules to bear in mind:

- ✔ A chord is major by default (which means that the third is major by default). Hence, when speaking of a chord, '*C*' is the same as saying '*C major*'.

- ✔ A fifth isn't mentioned in the name of the chord when it is **perfect**. (You don't say '*C major perfect fifth*', simply '*C major*' or '*C*'.)

- ✔ A seventh is minor by default:

    - '*C seventh*' means '*C major with a minor seventh*'.

    - '*C major seventh*' means '*C major with a major seventh*' (since a chord is major by default, this is not expressed and the term major then applies to the seventh).

    - '*C minor seventh*' means '*C minor with a minor seventh*' (a seventh being minor by default, it is not expressed and the term minor then applies to the third).

> ✔ No mention is made of the fact that an embellishment is **major** or **perfect**: if nothing is indicated, it is so (major or minor) by default. (You say '*C thirteenth*' not '*C major thirteenth*'. However, you do say '*C minor thirteenth*'.)

Here now are the notations used in addition to the usual notation to identify a chord in full (as an example we use the C chord – but this system can be applied to all keys):

Cmaj = C major (also expressed as C, CM): *C, E, G*

Cmin = C minor (also expressed as C-, Cm): *C, E♭, G*

C6 = C major with a major sixth: *C, E, G, A*

Cmin6 = C minor 6 = C minor with a major sixth: *C, E♭, G, A*

Csus4 = C suspended 4 = C major where the 3rd is replaced by the perfect fourth: *C, F, G*

C5 = Root and fifth, no third: *C, G*

C⁺ = augmented C (also expressed as Caug, C^{5+}) = C major with an augmented fifth: *C, E♭, G♯*

C⁰ = diminished C (also expressed as 'Cdim') = C minor with a diminished fifth: *C, E♭, G♭*

C^M7 = C major, major seventh (also expressed as C^Δ, C^maj7): *C, E, G, B*

C⁷ = C major, minor seventh: *C, E, G, B♭*

Cmin⁷ = C minor, minor seventh (also expressed as C-⁷, Cm⁷): *C, E♭, G, B♭*

Cmin$^{7\flat 5}$ = C minor with a diminished fifth and a minor seventh (also expressed as C$^{\AE}$, Cm$^{7\flat 5}$): *C, E$\flat$, G$\flat$, B$\flat$*

C$^{\text{sus4 }7}$ = C suspended 4, minor seventh: *C, F, G, B$\flat$*

C^{+7} = augmented C, minor seventh (also expressed as Caug^7):*C, E, G$\sharp$, B$\flat$*

C$^{\text{O7}}$ = diminished C, diminished seventh (one semitone below the minor seventh) (also expressed as Cdim^7): *C, E$\flat$, G$\flat$, B$\flat\flat$ (= A)*

Cmin$^{\text{maj7}}$ = C minor, major seventh (also expressed as Cm$^{\triangle}$): *C, E$\flat$, G, B*

Cadd^9 = C major, major ninth: *C, E, G, D*

C$^{\text{sus9}}$ = C major where the third is replaced by the major 9th: *C, G, D*

C$^{\text{M7 }9}$ = C major, major seventh, major ninth: *C, E, G, B, D*

C$^{7\ 9}$ = C major, minor seventh, major ninth: *C, E, G, B$\flat$, D*

C$^{7\flat 9}$ = C major, minor seventh, minor ninth: *C, E, G, B$\flat$, D$\flat$*

C$^{7\sharp 9}$ = C major, minor seventh, augmented ninth: *C, E, G, B$\flat$, D$\sharp$*

C$^{\text{sus4 }7\ 9}$ = C suspended 4, minor seventh, major ninth: *C, F, G, B$\flat$, D*

Cmin$^{7\ 9}$ = C minor, minor seventh, major ninth: *C, E$\flat$, G, B$\flat$, D*

C$^{\text{M7}\sharp 11}$ = C major, major seventh, augmented eleventh: *C, E, G, B, F$\sharp$*

$C^{7\sharp 11}$ = C major, minor seventh, augmented eleventh: *C, E, G, B♭, F♯*

Cmin$^{7\,11}$ = C minor, minor seventh, perfect: *C, E♭, G, B♭, F*

$C^{M7\,13}$ = C major, major seventh, major thirteenth: *C, E, G, B, A*

$C^{7\,13}$ = C major, minor seventh, major thirteenth: *C, E, G, B♭, A*

$C^{7♭13}$ = C major, minor seventh, minor thirteenth: *C, E, G, B♭, A♭*

The above list contains the chords which appear in this book. Naturally enough, it would be impossible to cover the entire list of chords which is almost endless. Nevertheless, this list provides you with a solid basis and the necessary know-how to enable you to work out a whole host of more complex chords which aren't in this book.

Defining Some Technical Terms

Here are some frequently used technical terms which will come in handy when working on your guitar chords.

Voicing: Voicing is a way of arranging the notes in a chord. Although you'll often find the root at the bottom (the lowest note of the chord), it's not all that unusual, particularly on the guitar, to have the other notes of the chord in a more or less haphazard arrangement.

For example, in the case of a C^{M7} chord, you could have *C* (root) at the bottom, followed by *B* (seventh), then *E* (third) and lastly *G* (fifth). This is what is known as a voicing.

Another voicing could be: C^{M7}, the arrangement containing: *C, E, B, G.*

Fingering: The fingering of a chord is the way in which the fingers are placed on the neck of the guitar to form this chord.

Playing an 'open' chord: This is done by playing the chord without pressing down on all of the strings.

Being a Canny Reader

Under each chord name you'll find a summary of the relevant notes (for example, Root = C; maj 3rd = E; 5th = G).

In some cases, you can find notes carrying double flats or double sharps, which could throw you somewhat.

Take the chord *C* diminished 7 (Cdim7) on page 40, where you read: dim 7th = B$^{\flat\flat}$.

This isn't a mistake: in effect, a B with two flats diminishes that note twice by one semitone. On the guitar, that would bring you to *A.*

However, if you were to count as you did earlier, you'd find that the 7th of *C* is *B* and that *A* is the sixth! In current parlance among musicians, the tendency would be not to mention the double flats and sharps. In the case of our example, you'd no longer say that the diminished 7th of *C* is *A.* However, according to the rules of theory, it is indeed a *B double flat.*

In order to avoid having too many *double flats/sharps* and making the reading of this book too confusing, some sharp or flat keys (for example, C$^{\sharp}$/D$^{\flat}$) are referred to either as sharp or flat: for example, $B\flat$ involves far fewer double flats than $A\sharp$ has double sharps, which means that it is easier to read.

You'll notice that we've removed the **perfect** fifth from certain chords. Take $C7^9$ for example (page 43) which consists of the notes C, E, $B\flat$, D. In theory, this chord also includes the perfect fifth (G), but the guitar is made in such a way that it would be extremely difficult, and indeed occasionally impossible, to position the fingers to be able to play all these notes.

Where perfect, the fifth doesn't contribute any essential colour to the chord, unlike the root/third/seventh. It would, therefore, be possible to remove it, if need be, so as to be able to place other notes in the chord.

Becoming an Efficient Musician

Some chords might discourage you at first either because they require a particular position of the fingers or greater pressure. Don't throw in the towel! The chords contained in this book are all achievable and fun to play. With a little effort, you'll soon find that you have no further difficulty in playing them.

You'll notice that if you follow the logic of this book, some chords are missing, such as the $^\varnothing9$ or M7 11 chords and more. Although occurring less frequently, these missing chords do still exist. Moreover, they refer to some very specific and quite complex rules of theory so we didn't consider it necessary to include them in this book.

It is (unfortunately!) possible to play some notes and chords on the guitar without really 'understanding' what you're doing, rather like a robot. Whether you use this book as a dictionary or as a method, we recommend that you listen carefully to each chord that you work on. Try to sing the notes of the chord, to recognise its colours. This enables you to progress much more quickly and your pleasure in making music will only be the greater for it.

Lastly, we can't stress enough how important it is to devise and try out your own chords. There's no such thing as a 'bad' chord. It's all a question of taste, context and artistic preference.

Part I
C-family Chords

Cmaj (M) *

Root = C; maj 3rd = E; 5th = G

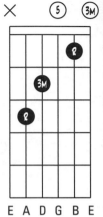

Cmaj (M) *

Root = C; maj 3rd = E; 5th = G

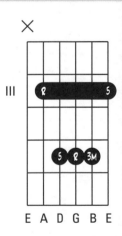

Cmaj (M)*

Root = C; maj 3rd = E; 5th = G

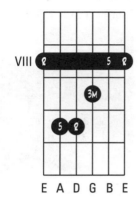

Cmin (m, -)*

Root = C; min 3rd = E♭; 5th = G

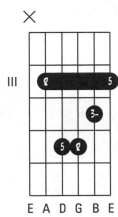

In order to obtain a minor chord, the major 3rd of the major chord needs to be lowered by one semitone (1 fret) to make it minor.

Cmin (m, -)*

Root = C; min 3rd = E♭; 5th = G

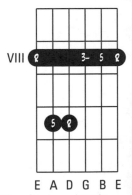

In order to obtain a minor chord, the major 3rd of the major chord needs to be lowered by one semitone (1 fret) to make it minor.

C6

Root = C; maj 3rd = E; maj 6th = A

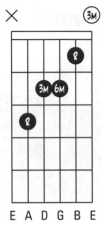

E A D G B E

For this form of 6th chord on the guitar, we have raised the 5th of the major chord situated on the G string by one tone (2 frets) in order to obtain the major 6th.

C6

Root = C; maj 3rd = E; 5th = G; maj 6th = A

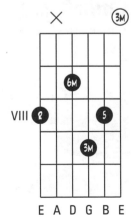

E A D G B E

For this form of 6th chord on the guitar, we have lowered the root of the major chord situated on the D string by one and a half tones (3 frets) in order to obtain the major 6th.

Cmin6 *(m6, -6)*

Root = C; min 3rd = E♭; 5th = G; maj 6th = A

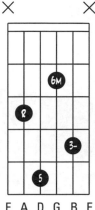

E A D G B E

For this form of min6 chord on the guitar, we have lowered the root of the minor chord situated on the G string by one and a half tones (3 frets) in order to obtain the major 6th.

Cmin6 *(m6, -6)*

Root = C; min 3rd = E♭; 5th = G; maj 6th = A

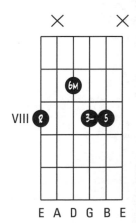

VIII

E A D G B E

For this form of min6 chord on the guitar, we have lowered the root of the minor chord situated on the D string by one and a half tones (3 frets) in order to obtain the major 6th.

Csus4 *

Root = C; 4th = F; 5th = G

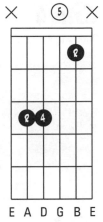

E A D G B E

In order to obtain a sus4 chord, raise the 3rd of a major chord by one semitone (1 fret) so that it becomes the 4th. A sus4 chord does not include a 3rd: it is neither major nor minor.

Csus4

Root = C; 4th = F; 5th = G

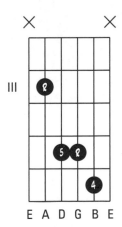

E A D G B E

In order to obtain a sus4 chord, raise the 3rd of a major chord by one semitone (1 fret) so that it becomes the 4th. A sus4 chord does not include a 3rd: it is neither major nor minor.

Csus4

Root = C; 4th = F; 5th = G

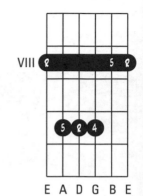

VIII

E A D G B E

If you have any difficulty in placing this chord, you need not play the lowest 5th (on the A string), as it can be found again on the B string.

C5 *

Root = C; 5th = G

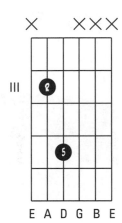

'5' chords consist of only 2 notes: the root and the 5th. Used a lot in rock and heavy metal, they are also referred to as *power chords*.

C5 *

Root = C; 5th = G

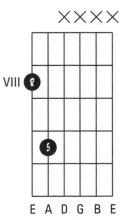

'5' chords consist of only 2 notes: the root and the 5th. Used a lot in rock and heavy metal, they are also referred to as *power chords*.

Caug ($^{\#5}$, +, $^{5+}$)

Root = C; maj 3rd = E; 5$^{th}\#$ = G$\#$

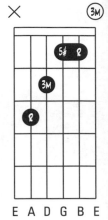

E A D G B E

An augmented chord is a major chord in which the 5th has been raised by one semitone (1 fret).

Caug ($^{\#5}$, +, $^{5+}$)

Root = C; maj 3rd = E; 5$^{th}\#$ = G$\#$

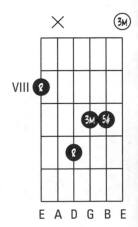

E A D G B E

If you have any difficulty in placing this chord, you need only play the 3 highest notes of the chord (the base – in this case the root – may be omitted as it is repeated an octave higher).

Cdim (°)

Root = C; min 3rd = E♭; 5th♭ = G♭

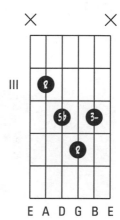

A diminished chord is a major chord in which, with the exception of the root, all the notes have been lowered by one semitone (1 fret).

Cdim (°)

Root = C; min 3rd = E♭; 5th♭ = G♭

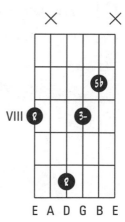

If you have any difficulty in placing this chord, you need only play the 3 highest notes of the chord (the base – in this case the root – may be omitted as it is repeated an octave higher).

C^{M7} ($7M$, $Maj7$, $7Maj$, $\triangle$) *

Root = C; maj 3rd = E; 5th = G; maj 7th = B

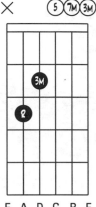

E A D G B E

For this form of ^{M7} chord on the guitar, we have lowered the root of the major chord situated on the B string by one semitone (1 fret) in order to obtain the major 7th.

C^{M7} ($7M$, $Maj7$, $7Maj$, $\triangle$)

Root = C; maj 3rd = E; 5th = G; maj 7th = B

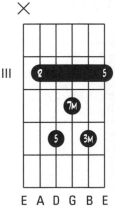

III

E A D G B E

For this form of ^{M7} chord on the guitar, we have lowered the root of the major chord situated on the G string by one semitone (1 fret) in order to obtain the major 7th.

C^{M7} (7M, Maj7, 7Maj, △)

Root = C; maj 3rd = E; 5th = G; maj 7th = B

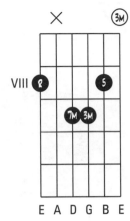

For this form of M7 chord on the guitar, we have lowered the root of the major chord situated on the D string by one semitone (1 fret) in order to obtain the major 7th.

C7

Root = C; maj 3rd = E; min 7th = B♭

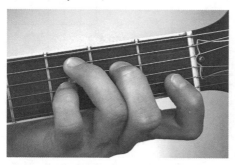

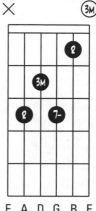

Please note that for this form of, currently used, 7th chord we have removed the 5th of the major chord on the G string so as to be able place the minor 7th.

C7

Root = C; maj 3rd = E; 5th = G; min 7th = B♭

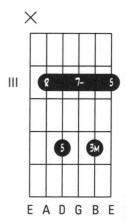

In order to obtain the 7th chord, the major 7th of the M7 chord must be lowered by one semitone (1 fret) so that it becomes minor.

C7

Root = C; maj 3rd = E; 5th = G min; 7th = B$^\flat$

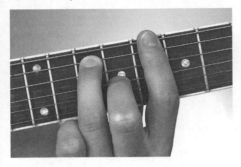

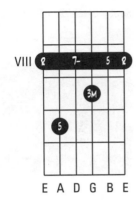

VIII ℛ 7- 5 ℛ

3M

5

E A D G B E

In order to obtain the 7th chord, the major 7th of the ^{M7} chord must be lowered by one semitone (1 fret) so that it becomes minor.

Cmin7 (m7, -7)

Root = C; min 3rd = E♭; 5th = G; min 7th = B♭

Root = C; min 3rd = E$^\flat$; 5th = G; min 7th = B$^\flat$

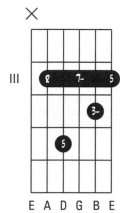

III

E A D G B E

In order to obtain a min7 chord, the major 3rd of the 7th chord must be lowered by one semitone (1 fret) so that it becomes minor.

Cmin7 (m7, -7)

Root = C; min 3rd = E$^\flat$; 5th = G; min 7th = B$^\flat$

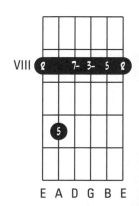

VIII

E A D G B E

In order to obtain a min7 chord, the major 3rd of the 7th chord must be lowered by one semitone (1 fret) so that it becomes minor.

Cmin7♭5 *(m7♭5, -7♭5, ∅)*

Root = C; min 3rd = E♭; 5th♭ = G♭; min 7th = B♭

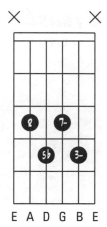

E A D G B E

In order to obtain a min7♭5 chord, the 5th of the min7 chord must be lowered by one semitone (1 fret) so that it becomes a flat 5th (also known as a *diminished 5th*).

Cmin7♭5 *(m7♭5, -7♭5, ∅)*

Root = C; min 3rd = E♭; 5th♭ = G♭; min 7th = B♭

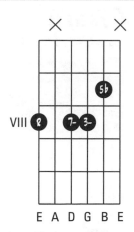

E A D G B E

In order to obtain a min7♭5 chord, the 5th of the min7 chord must be lowered by one semitone (1 fret) so that it becomes a flat 5th (also known as a *diminished 5th*).

C7sus4

Root = C; 4th = F; 5th = G; min 7th = B♭

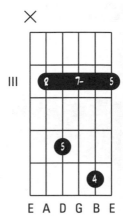

In order to obtain a 7sus4 chord, raise the major 3rd of the 7th chord by one semitone (1 fret) so that it becomes the 4th. A 7sus4 chord does not include a 3rd: it is neither major nor minor.

C7sus4

Root = C; 4th = F; 5th = G; min 7th = B♭

If you have any difficulty in placing this chord, you need not play the lowest 5th (on the A string), as it can be found again on the B string.

Caug7 *(7$^{\sharp 5}$, +7)*

Root = C; maj 3rd = E; 5$^{th\sharp}$ = G$^{\sharp}$; min 7th = B$^{\flat}$

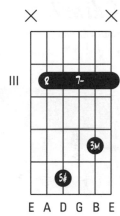

An aug7 chord is a 7th chord in which the 5th has been raised by one semitone (1 fret). Please note that even if you press on the high E because of the barre chord, it should not be played.

Caug7 *(7$^{\sharp 5}$, +7)*

Root = C; maj 3rd = E; 5$^{th\sharp}$ = G$^{\sharp}$; min 7th = B$^{\flat}$

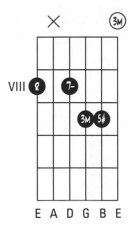

An aug7 chord is a 7th chord in which the 5th has been raised by one semitone (1 fret).

Cdim7 (°7)

Root = C; min 3rd = E$^\flat$; 5th$^\flat$ = G$^\flat$; min 7th = B$^{\flat\flat}$(A)

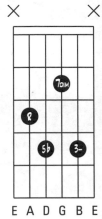

E A D G B E

A dim chord is a 7th chord in which, with the exception of the root, all the notes have been raised by one semitone (1 fret).

Cdim7 (°7)

Root = C; min 3rd = E$^\flat$; 5th$^\flat$ = G$^\flat$; min 7th = B$^{\flat\flat}$(A)

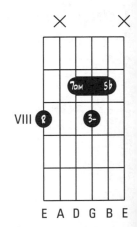

VIII

E A D G B E

A dim chord is a 7th chord in which, with the exception of the root, all the notes have been raised by one semitone (1 fret).

$Cmin^{M7}$ (-M7, min△, -△)

Root = C; min 3rd = E♭; 5th = G; maj 7th = B

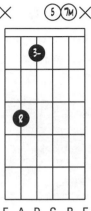

In order to obtain a minM7 chord, the minor 7th of the min7 chord must be raised by one semitone (1 fret) so that it becomes major.

$Cmin^{M7}$ (-M7, min△, -△)

Root = C; min 3rd = E♭; 5th = G; maj 7th = B

In order to obtain a minM7 chord, the minor 7th of the min7 chord must be raised by one semitone (1 fret) so that it becomes major.

Csus9

Root = C; 5th = G; 9th = D

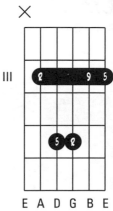

In order to obtain a sus9 chord, the major 3rd of the major chord must be lowered by one tone (2 frets) so that it becomes the 9th. A sus9 chord does not include a 3rd: it is neither major nor minor.

Cadd9

Root = C; maj 3rd = E; 5th = G; 9th = D

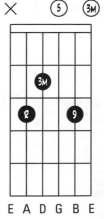

An add9 chord is a major chord to which a 9th has been added.

$C^{M7\ 9}$ *(Maj7 9, Δ9)*

Root = C; maj 3rd = E; maj 7th = B; 9th = D

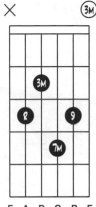

In order to play this form of $^{M7\ 9}$ chord on the guitar, we have removed the 5th of the ^{M7} chord situated on the D string so as to be able to place the 9th.

$C7^{\ 9}$

Root = C; maj 3rd = E; min 7th = B♭; 9th = D

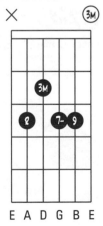

In order to play this form of 7 9 chord on the guitar, we have removed the 5th of the 7th chord situated on the D string so as to be able to place the 9th.

C7^{b9}

Root = C; maj 3rd = E; min 7th = B^b; 9^{thb} = D^b

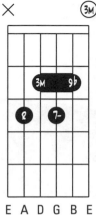

E A D G B E

In order to play this form of 7^{b9} chord on the guitar, we have removed the 5th of the 7th chord situated on the D string so as to be able to place the 9^{thb}.

C7$^{\#9}$

Root = C; maj 3rd = E; min 7th = B^b; 9$^{th\#}$ = D$^\#$

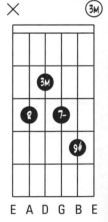

E A D G B E

In order to play this form of 7$^{\#9}$ chord on the guitar, we have removed the 5th of the 7th chord situated on the D string so as to be able to place the 9$^{th\#}$.

C7sus4⁹

Root = C; 4ᵗʰ = F; 5ᵗʰ = G; min 7ᵗʰ = B♭; 9ᵗʰ = D

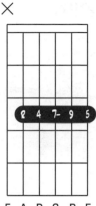

E A D G B E

In order to obtain a 7sus4⁹ chord, raise the major 3ʳᵈ of the 7⁹ chord by one semitone (1 fret) so that it becomes a 4ᵗʰ. A 7sus4⁹ chord does not include a 3ʳᵈ: it is neither major nor minor.

Cmin7⁹ *(m7⁹, -7⁹)*

Root = C; min 3ʳᵈ = E♭; min 7ᵗʰ = B♭; 9ᵗʰ = D

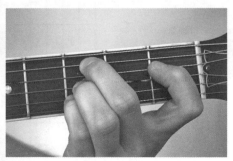

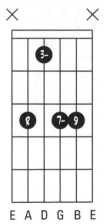

E A D G B E

In order to play this form of min7⁹ chord on the guitar, we have removed the 5ᵗʰ of the min7 chord situated on the D string so as to be able to place the 9ᵗʰ.

$C^{M7\sharp 11}$ $(Maj7\sharp 11, \triangle\sharp 11)$

Root = C; maj 3rd = E; maj 7th = B; $11^{th}\sharp$ = F$\sharp$

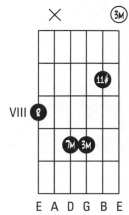

In order to play this form of $^{M7}\sharp 11$ chord on the guitar, we have removed the 5th of the ^{M7} chord situated on the B string so as to be able to place the $11^{th}\sharp$.

$C7^{\sharp 11}$

Root = C; maj 3rd = E; min 7th = B$\flat$; $11^{th}\sharp$ = F$\sharp$

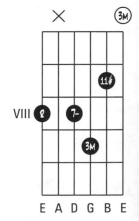

In order to play this form of $7^{\sharp 11}$ chord on the guitar, we have removed the 5th of the 7th chord situated on the B string so as to be able to place the $11^{th}\sharp$.

Cmin7¹¹ (*m7¹¹*, *-7¹¹*)

Root = C; min 3rd = E$^\flat$; min 7th = B$^\flat$; 11th = F

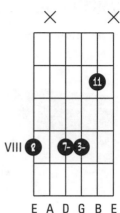

In order to play this form of min7¹¹ chord on the guitar, we have removed the 5th of the min7 chord situated on the B string so as to be able to place the perfect 11th.

$C^{M7\ 13}$ ($^{Maj7\ 13}$, $\triangle\ 13$)

Root = C; maj 3rd = E; maj 7th = B; maj 13th = A

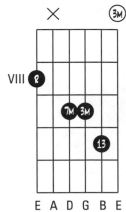

E A D G B E

In order to play this form of $^{M7\ 13}$ chord on the guitar, we have removed the 5th of the ^{M7} chord situated on the B string so as to be able to place the major 13th.

$C7^{\ 13}$

Root = C; maj 3rd = E; min 7th = B$^\flat$; maj 13th = A

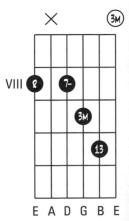

E A D G B E

In order to play this form of 7^{13} chord on the guitar, we have removed the 5th of the 7th chord situated on the B string so as to be able to place the major 13th.

C7$^{\flat 13}$

Root = C; maj 3rd = E; min 7th = B$^{\flat}$; (min) 13$^{th\flat}$ = A$^{\flat}$

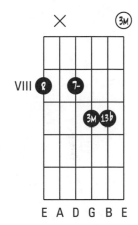

In order to play this form of 7$^{\flat 13}$ chord on the guitar, we have removed the 5th of the 7th chord situated on the B string so as to be able to place the minor 13th (13$^{th\flat}$).

Part II
D♭/ C♯-family Chords

D♭/C# maj (M) *

Root = D♭; maj 3rd = F; 5th = A♭

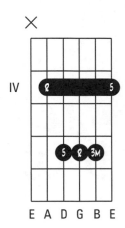

IV

E A D G B E

D♭/C# maj (M) *

Root = D♭; maj 3rd = F; 5th = A♭

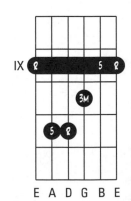

IX

E A D G B E

D♭/C♯ min (m, -)*

Root = D♭; min 3rd = F♭; 5th = A♭

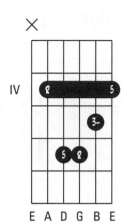

In order to obtain a minor chord, the major 3rd of the major chord must be lowered by one semitone (1 fret) so that it becomes minor.

D♭/C♯ min (m, -)*

Root = D♭; min 3rd = F♭; 5th = A♭

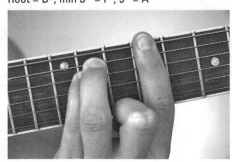
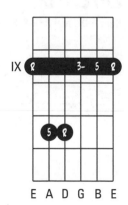

In order to obtain a minor chord, the major 3rd of the major chord must be lowered by one semitone (1 fret) so that it becomes minor.

D♭/C♯ 6

Root = D♭; maj 3rd = F; maj 6th = B♭

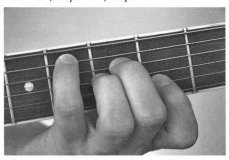

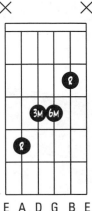

E A D G B E

In order play this form of 6th chord on the guitar, we have removed the 5th of the major chord so as to be able to place the major 6th.

D♭/C♯ 6

Root = D♭; maj 3rd = F; 5th = A♭; maj 6th = B♭

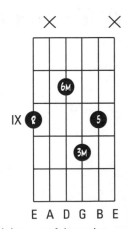

IX

E A D G B E

For this form of 6th chord on the guitar, we have lowered the root of the major chord situated on the D string by one and a half tones (3 frets) in order to obtain the major 6th.

D♭/C♯ *min6* (m6, -6)

Root = D♭; min 3rd = F♭ (E); 5th = A♭; maj 6th = B♭

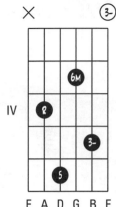

For this form of min6 chord on the guitar, we have lowered the root of the minor chord situated on the G string by one and a half tones (3 frets) in order to obtain the major 6th.

D♭/C♯ *min6* (m6, -6)

Root = D♭; min 3rd = F♭ (E); 5th = A♭; maj 6th = B♭

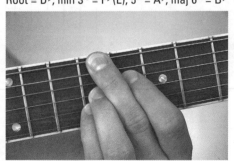

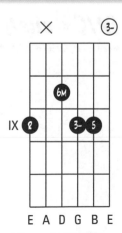

For this form of min6 chord on the guitar, we have lowered the root of the minor chord situated on the D string by one and a half tones (3 frets) in order to obtain the major 6th.

D♭/C♯ sus4

Root = D♭; 4th = G♭; 5th = A♭

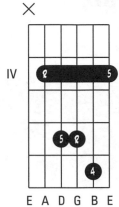

X

IV

E A D G B E

In order to obtain a sus4 chord, raise the 3rd of a major chord by one semitone (1 fret) so that it becomes the 4th. A sus4 chord does not include a 3rd: it is neither major nor minor.

D♭/C♯ sus4

Root = D♭; 4th = G♭; 5th = A♭

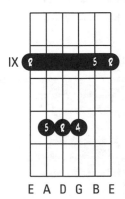

IX

E A D G B E

TIP

If you have any difficulty in placing this chord, you need not play the lowest 5th (on the A string), as it can be found again on the B string.

D♭/C♯ **5** *

Root = D♭; 5th = A♭

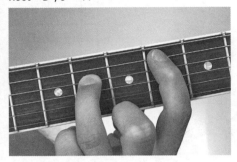

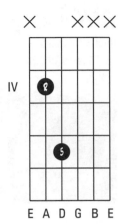

The '5' chords consist of only 2 notes: the root and the 5th. Used a lot in rock and heavy metal, they are also referred to as *power chords*.

D♭/C♯ **5** *

Root = D♭; 5th = A♭

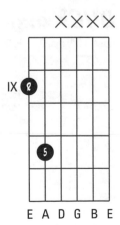

The '5' chords consist of only 2 notes: the root and the 5th. Used a lot in rock and heavy metal, they are also referred to as *power chords*.

D♭/C♯ aug (♯5, +, 5+)

Root = D♭; maj 3rd = F; 5th♯ = A

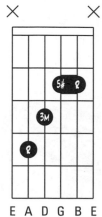

× ×

E A D G B E

An augmented chord is a major chord in which the 5th has been raised by one semitone (1 fret).

D♭/C♯ aug (♯5, +, 5+)

Root = D♭; maj 3rd = F; 5th♯ = A

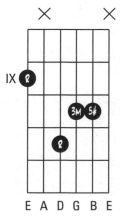

× ×

IX

E A D G B E

If you have any difficulty in placing this chord, you need only play the 3 highest notes of the chord (the base – in this case the root – may be omitted as it is repeated an octave higher).

D♭/C♯ 5 dim (°)

Root = D♭; min 3rd = F♭(E); 5th♭ = A♭♭ (G)

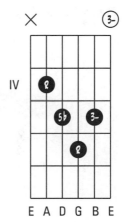

A diminished chord is a major chord in which, with the exception of the root, all the notes have been lowered by one semitone (1 fret).

D♭/C♯ dim (°)

Root = D♭; min 3rd = F♭(E); 5th♭ = A♭♭ (G)

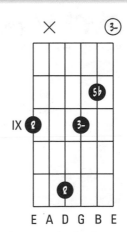

TIP

If you have any difficulty in placing this chord, you need only play the 3 highest notes of the chord (the base – in this case the root – may be omitted as it is repeated an octave higher).

D♭/C♯ ᴹ⁷ ₍₇ₘ, ₘₐⱼ₇, ₇ₘₐⱼ, △₎

Root = D♭; maj 3ʳᵈ = F; 5ᵗʰ = A♭; maj 7ᵗʰ = C

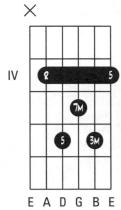

For this form of ᴹ⁷ chord on the guitar, we have lowered the root of the major chord situated on the G string by one semitone (1 fret) in order to obtain the major 7ᵗʰ.

D♭/C♯ ᴹ⁷ ₍₇ₘ, ₘₐⱼ₇, ₇ₘₐⱼ, △₎

Root = D♭; maj 3ʳᵈ = F; 5ᵗʰ = A♭; maj 7ᵗʰ = C

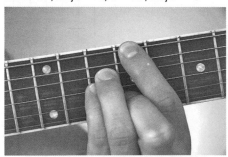

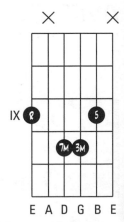

For this form of ᴹ⁷ chord on the guitar, we have lowered the root of the major chord situated on the G string by one semitone (1 fret) in order to obtain the major 7ᵗʰ.

D♭/C♯ 7 *

Root = D♭; maj 3rd = F; min 7th = C♭ (B)

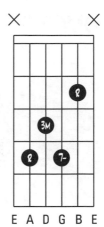

E A D G B E

Please note that for this form of, currently used, 7th chord we have removed the 5th of the major chord so as to be able place the minor 7th.

D♭/C♯ 7

Root = D♭; maj 3rd = F; 5th = A♭; min 7th = C♭ (B)

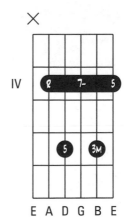

E A D G B E

In order to obtain the 7th chord, the major 7th of the M7 chord must be lowered by one semitone (1 fret) so that it becomes minor.

D♭/C♯ 7

Root = D♭; maj 3rd = F; 5th = A♭; min 7th = C♭ (B)

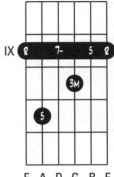

IX

E A D G B E

In order to obtain the 7th chord, the major 7th of the M7 chord must be lowered by one semitone (1 fret) so that it becomes minor.

D♭/C♯ min7 (m7, -7)

Root = D♭; min 3ʳᵈ = F♭ (E); 5ᵗʰ = A♭; min 7ᵗʰ = C♭ (B)

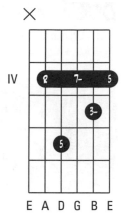

In order to obtain a min7 chord, the major 3ʳᵈ of the 7ᵗʰ chord must be lowered
by one semitone (1 fret) so that it becomes minor.

D♭/C♯ min7 (m7, -7)

Root = D♭; min 3ʳᵈ = F♭ (E); 5ᵗʰ = A♭; min 7ᵗʰ = C♭ (B)

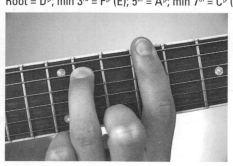

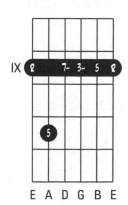

In order to obtain a min7 chord, the major 3ʳᵈ of the 7ᵗʰ chord must be lowered
by one semitone (1 fret) so that it becomes minor.

D♭/C♯ min7♭5 (m7♭5, -7♭5, ∅)

Root = D♭; min 3rd = F♭ (E); 5th♭ = A♭; min 7th = C♭ (B)

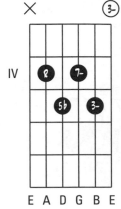

IV

E A D G B E

In order to obtain a min7♭5 chord, the 5th of the min7 chord must be lowered by one semitone (1 fret) so that it becomes flat 5th (also referred to as *diminished 5th*).

D♭/C♯ min7♭5 (m7♭5, -7♭5, ∅)

Root = D♭; min 3rd = F♭ (E); 5th♭ = A♭; min 7th = C♭ (B)

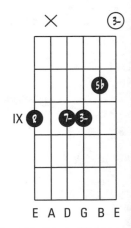

IX

E A D G B E

In order to obtain a min7♭5 chord, the 5th of the min7 chord must be lowered by one semitone (1 fret) so that it becomes flat 5th (also referred to as *diminished 5th*).

D♭/C♯ 7sus4

Root = D♭; 4th = G♭; 5th♭ = A♭; min 7th = C♭ (B)

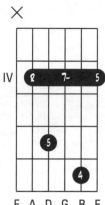

E A D G B E

In order to obtain a 7sus4 chord, augment the major 3rd of the 7th chord by one semitone (1 fret) so that it becomes the 4th. A 7sus4 chord does not include a 3rd: it is neither major nor minor.

D♭/C♯ 7sus4

Root = D♭; 4th = G♭; 5th♭ = A♭; min 7th = C♭ (B)

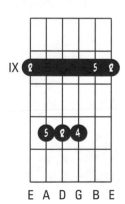

E A D G B E

TIP

If you have any difficulty in placing this chord, you need not play the lowest 5th (on the A string), as it can be found again on the B string.

D♭/C♯ aug7 (7#5, +7)

Root = D♭; maj 3rd = F; 5th# = A; min 7th = C♭ (B)

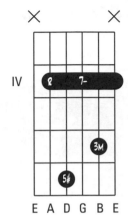

An aug7 chord is the 7th chord in which the 5th has been raised by one semitone (1 fret). Please note that even if you press on the high E because of the barre chord, that string should not be played.

D♭/C♯ aug7 (7#5, +7)

Root = D♭; maj 3rd = F; 5th# = A; min 7th = C♭ (B)

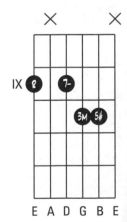

An aug7 chord is the 7th chord in which the 5th has been raised by one semitone (1 fret).

D♭/C♯ dim7 (°7)

Root = D♭; min 3rd = F♭ (E); 5th♭ = A♭♭ (G); dim 7th = C♭♭ (B♭)

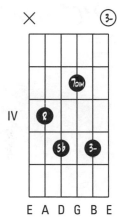

A dim chord is a 7th chord in which, with the exception of the root, all the notes have been lowered by one semitone (1 fret).

D♭/C♯ dim7 (°7)

Root = D♭; min 3rd = F♭ (E); 5th♭ = A♭♭ (G); dim 7th = C♭♭ (B♭)

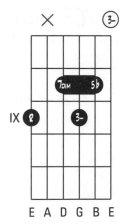

A dim chord is a 7th chord in which, with the exception of the root, all the notes have been lowered by one semitone (1 fret).

D♭/C♯ *min*^M7 (-^M7, *min*^△, -^△)

Root = D♭; min 3rd = F♭; 5th = A♭; maj 7th = C

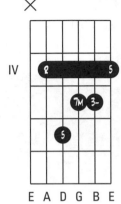

IV

E A D G B E

In order to obtain a min^M7 chord, the minor 7th of the min7 chord must be raised by one semitone (1 fret) so that it becomes major.

D♭/C♯ *min*^M7 (-^M7, *min*^△, -^△)

Root = D♭; min 3rd = F♭; 5th = A♭; maj 7th = C

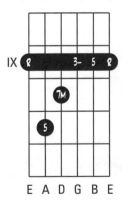

IX

E A D G B E

In order to obtain a min^M7 chord, the minor 7th of the min7 chord must be raised by one semitone (1 fret) so that it becomes major.

D♭/C♯ sus9

Root = D♭; 5th = A♭; 9th = E♭

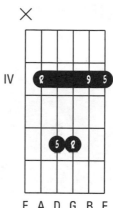

To obtain a sus9 chord, the major 3rd of the major chord needs to be lowered by one tone (2 frets) so that it becomes the 9th. A sus9 chord does not include a 3rd: it is neither major nor minor.

D♭/C♯ add9

Root = D♭; maj 3rd = F; 5th = A♭; 9th = E♭

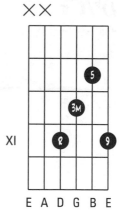

An add9 chord is a major chord to which a 9th has been added.

D♭/C# M7 9 *(Maj7 9, Δ9)*

Root = D♭; maj 3rd = F; maj 7th = C; 9th = E♭

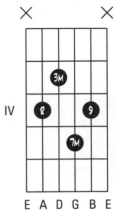

In order to play this form of M7chord on the guitar, we have removed the 5th of the M7chord situated on the D string so as to be able to place the 9th.

D♭/C# 7⁹

Root = D♭; maj 3rd = F; min 7th = C♭ (B); 9th = E♭

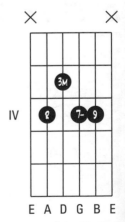

In order to play this form of 7⁹ chord on the guitar, we have removed the 5th of the 7th chord situated on the D string so as to be able to place the 9th.

D♭/C♯ 7♭9

Root = D♭; maj 3rd = F; min 7th = C♭ (B); 9th♭ = E♭♭ (D)

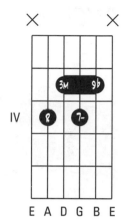

In order to play this form of 7♭9 chord on the guitar, we have removed the 5th of the 7 chord situated on the D string so as to be able to place the 9th♭.

D♭/C♯ 7♯9

Root = D♭; maj 3rd = F; min 7th = C♭ (B); 9th♯ = E

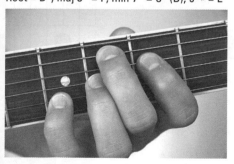

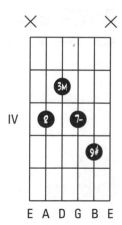

In order to play this form of 7♯9 chord on the guitar, we have removed the 5th of the 7 chord situated on the D string so as to be able to place the 9th♯.

D♭/C♯ 7sus4⁹

Root = D♭; 4ᵗʰ = G♭ ;5ᵗʰ = A♭; min 7ᵗʰ = C♭ (B); 9ᵗʰ = E♭

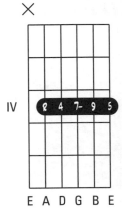

To obtain a 7sus4⁹ chord, raise the major 3ʳᵈ of the 7⁹ chord by one semitone (1 fret) so that it becomes the 4ᵗʰ. A 7sus4⁹ chord does not include a 3ʳᵈ: it is neither major nor minor.

D♭/C♯ min7⁹ (m7⁹, -7⁹)

Root = D♭; min 3ʳᵈ = F♭ (E); min 7ᵗʰ = C♭ (B); 9ᵗʰ = E♭

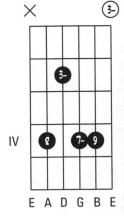

In order to play this form of 7⁹ chord on the guitar, we have removed the 5ᵗʰ of the min 7 chord situated on the D string so as to be able to place the 9ᵗʰ.

D♭/C♯ M7 ♯11 (Maj7♯11, △♯11)

Root = D♭; maj 3rd = F; maj 7th = C; 11th♯ = G

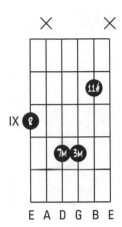

In order to play this form of M7♯11 chord on the guitar, we have removed the 5th of the M7 chord situated on the B string so as to be able to place the 11th♯.

D♭/C♯ 7♯11

Root = D♭; maj 3rd = F; min 7th = C♭ (B); 11th♯ = G

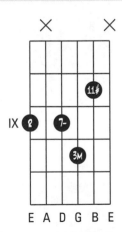

In order to play this form of 7♯11 chord on the guitar, we have removed the 5th of the 7th chord situated on the B string so as to be able to place the 11th♯.

D♭/C♯ min 7¹¹ (m7¹¹, -7¹¹)

Root = D♭; min 3rd = F♭ (E); min 7th = C♭ (B); 11th = G♭

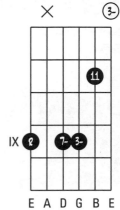

In order to play this form of min7¹¹ chord on the guitar, we have removed the 5th of the min7 chord situated on the B string so as to be able to place the perfect 11th.

D♭/C# *M713* (Maj7 13, △ 13)

Root = D♭; maj 3rd = F; maj 7th = C; 13th = B♭

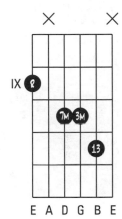

In order to play this form of M7 13 chord on the guitar, we have removed the 5th of the M7 chord situated on the B string so as to be able to place the major 13th.

D♭/C# *7¹³*

Root = D♭; maj 3rd = F; min 7th = C♭ (B); maj 13th = B♭

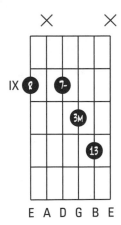

In order to play this form of 7¹³ chord on the guitar, we have removed the 5th of the 7th chord situated on the B string so as to be able to place the major 13th.

D♭/C♯ 7♭13

Root = D♭; maj 3rd = F; min 7th = C♭ (B); (min) 13th♭ = B♭♭ (A)

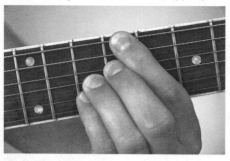

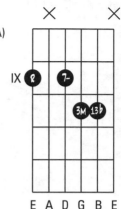

In order to play this form of 7♭13 chord on the guitar, we have removed the 5th of the 7th chord situated on the B string so as to be able to place the minor 13th (13th♭).

Part III
D-family Chords

Dmaj (M) *

Root = D; maj 3rd = F#; 5th = A

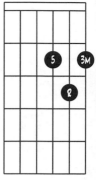

E A D G B E

Dmaj (M) *

Root = D; maj 3rd = F#; 5th = A

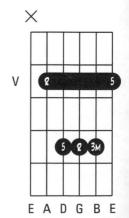

E A D G B E

Dmaj (M) *

Root = D; maj 3rd = F#; 5th = A

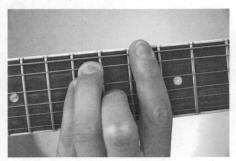

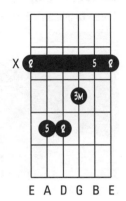

E A D G B E

Dmin (m, -) *

Root = D; min 3rd = F; 5th = A

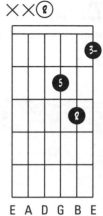

×× ℗

E A D G B E

To obtain a minor chord, the major 3rd of the major chord needs to be lowered by one semitone (1 fret) so that it becomes minor.

Dmin (m, -) *

Root = D; min 3rd = F; 5th = A

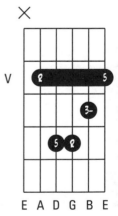

×

V

E A D G B E

To obtain a minor chord, the major 3rd of the major chord needs to be lowered by one semitone (1 fret) so that it becomes minor.

Dmin (m, -)*

Root = D; min 3rd = F; 5th = A

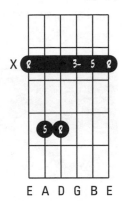

E A D G B E

To obtain a minor chord, the 3rd of the major chord needs to be lowered by one semitone (1 fret) so that it becomes minor.

D6

Root = D; maj 3rd = F$^{\sharp}$; 5th = A; maj 6th = B

For this form of 6th chord on the guitar, we have lowered the root of the major chord situated on the high E string by one and half tones (3 frets) in order to obtain the major 6th.

D6

Root = D; maj 3rd = F$^{\sharp}$; maj 6th = B

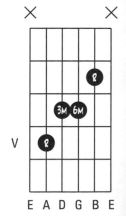

In order to play this form of 6th chord on the guitar, we have removed the 5th of the major chord so as to be able to place the major 6th.

D6

Root = D; maj 3rd = F#; 5th = A; maj 6th = B

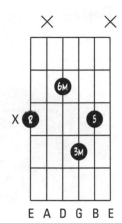

E A D G B E

For this form of 6th chord on the guitar, we have lowered the root of the major chord situated on the D string by one and half tones (3 frets) in order to obtain the major 6th.

Dmin6 (m6, -6)

Root = D; min 3rd = F; 5th = A; maj 6th = B

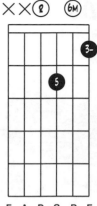

For this form of min6 chord on the guitar, we have lowered the root of the minor chord situated on the B string by one and half tones (3 frets) in order to obtain the major 6th.

Dmin6 (m6, -6)

Root = D; min 3rd = F; 5th = A; maj 6th = B

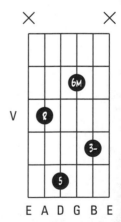

For this form of min6 chord on the guitar, we have lowered the root of the minor chord situated on the G string by one and half tones (3 frets) in order to obtain the major 6th.

Dmin6 *(m6, -6)*

Root = D; min 3rd = F; 5th = A; maj 6th = B

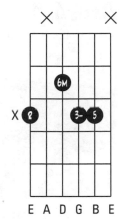

E A D G B E

For this form of min6 chord on the guitar, we have lowered the root of the minor chord situated on the D string by one and half tones (3 frets) in order to obtain the major 6th.

Dsus4 *

Root = D; 4th = G; 5th = A

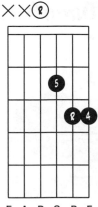

E A D G B E

To obtain a sus4 chord, raise the 3rd of a major chord by one semitone (1 fret) so that it becomes the 4th. A sus4 chord does not include a 3rd: it is neither major nor minor.

Dsus4

Root = D; 4th = G; 5th = A

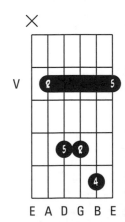

E A D G B E

To obtain a sus4 chord, raise the 3rd of a major chord by one semitone (1 fret) so that it becomes the 4th. A sus4 chord does not include a 3rd: it is neither major nor minor.

Dsus4

Root = D; 4th = G; 5th = A

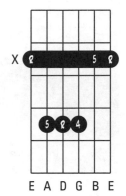

E A D G B E

If you have any difficulty in placing this chord, you need not play the lowest 5th (on the A string), as it can be found again on the B string.

D5 *

Root = D; 5th = A

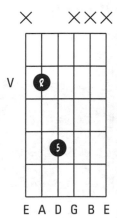

E A D G B E

'5' chords consist of only 2 notes: the root and the 5th. Used a lot in rock and heavy metal, they are also referred to as *power chords*.

D5 *

Root = C; 5th = A

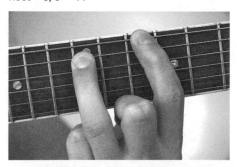

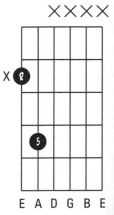

E A D G B E

'5' chords consist of only 2 notes: the root and the 5th. Used a lot in rock and heavy metal, they are also referred to as *power chords*.

Daug (#5, +, 5+)

Root = D; maj 3rd = F#; 5th# = A#

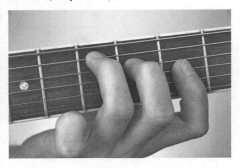

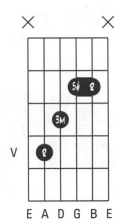

An augmented chord is a major chord in which the 5th has been raised by one semitone (1 fret).

Daug (#5, +, 5+)

Root = D; maj 3rd = F#; 5th# = A#

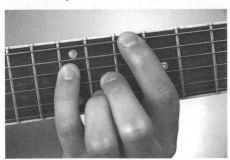

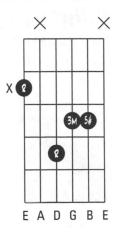

If you have any difficulty in placing this chord, you need only play the 3 highest notes of the chord (the base – in this case the root – may be omitted as it is repeated an octave higher).

Ddim (°)

Root = D; min 3rd = F; 5^{thb} = A^b

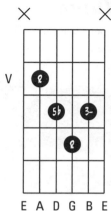

A diminished chord is a major chord in which, with the exception of the root, all the notes have been lowered by one semitone (1 fret).

Ddim (°)

Root = C; min 3rd = E^b; 5^{thb} = G^b

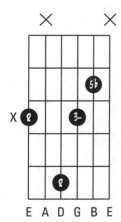

If you have any difficulty in placing this chord, you need only play the 3 highest notes of the chord (the base note – in this case the root – may be omitted as it is repeated an octave higher).

D^{M7} (7M, Maj7, 7Maj, △) *

Root = D; maj 3rd = F♯; 5th = A; maj 7th = C♯

E A D G B E

For this form of ^{M7} chord on the guitar, we have lowered the root of the major chord situated on the B string by one semitone (1 fret) in order to obtain the major 7th.

D^{M7} (7M, Maj7, 7Maj, △)

Root = D; maj 3rd = F♯; 5th = A; maj 7th = C♯

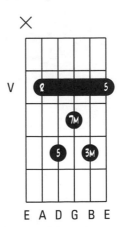

E A D G B E

For this form of ^{M7} chord on the guitar, we have lowered the root of the major chord situated on the G string by one semitone (1 fret) in order to obtain the major 7th.

D^{M7} (7M, Maj7, 7Maj, △)

Root = D; maj 3rd = F#; 5th = A; maj 7th = C#

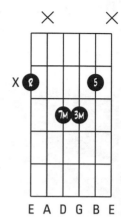

E A D G B E

For this form of ^{M7} chord on the guitar, we have lowered the root of the major chord situated on the B string by one semitone (1 fret) in order to obtain the major 7th.

D7 *

Root = D; maj 3rd = F#; 5th = A; min 7th = C

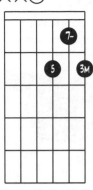

E A D G B E

To obtain the 7th chord, the major 7th of the ^{M7} chord needs to be lowered by one semitone (1 fret) so that it becomes minor.

D7 *

Root = D; maj 3rd = F#; 5th = A; min 7th = C

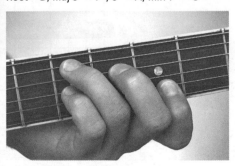

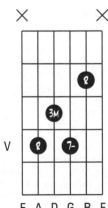

E A D G B E

Please note that for this form of, currently used, 7th chord we have removed the 5th of the major chord so as to be able place the minor 7th.

D7

Root = D; maj 3ʳᵈ = F♯; 5ᵗʰ = A; min 7ᵗʰ = C

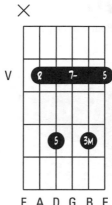

To obtain the 7ᵗʰ chord, the major 7ᵗʰ of the ᴹ⁷ chord needs to be lowered by one semitone (1 fret) so that it becomes minor.

D7

Root = D; maj 3ʳᵈ = F♯; 5ᵗʰ = A; min 7ᵗʰ = C

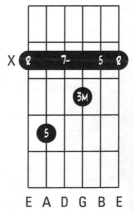

To obtain the 7ᵗʰ chord, the major 7ᵗʰ of the ᴹ⁷ chord needs to be lowered by one semitone (1 fret) so that it becomes minor.

Dmin7 (m7, -7)*

Root = D; min 3rd = F; 5th = A; min 7th = C

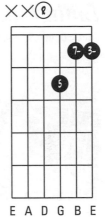

To obtain a min7 chord, the major 3rd of the 7th chord needs to be lowered by one semitone (1 fret) so that it becomes minor.

Dmin7 (m7, -7)

Root = D; min 3rd = F; 5th = A; min 7th = C

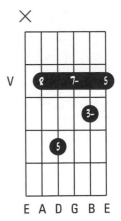

To obtain a min7 chord, the major 3rd of the 7th chord needs to be lowered by one semitone (1 fret) so that it becomes minor.

Dmin7 *(m7, -7)*

Root = D; min 3rd = F; 5th = A; min 7th = C

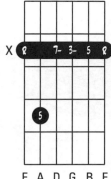

X

7- 3- 5

5

E A D G B E

To obtain a min7 chord, the major 3rd of the 7th chord needs to be lowered by one semitone (1 fret) so that it becomes minor.

Dmin 7♭5 (m7♭5, -7♭5, ∅)

Root = D; min 3rd = F; 5th♭ = A♭; min 7th = C

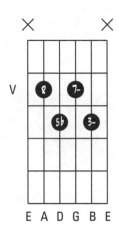

E A D G B E

In order to obtain a min7♭5 chord, the 5th of the min7 chord must be lowered by one semitone (1 fret) so that it becomes a flat 5th (also known as a *diminished 5th*).

Dmin 7♭5 (m7♭5, -7♭5, ∅)

Root = D; min 3rd = F; 5th♭ = A♭; min 7th = C

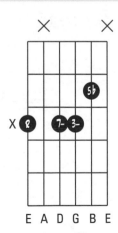

E A D G B E

In order to obtain a min7♭5 chord, the 5th of the min7 chord must be lowered by one semitone (1 fret) so that it becomes a flat 5th (also known as a *diminished 5th*).

D7sus4

Root = D; 4th = G; 5th = A; min 7th = C

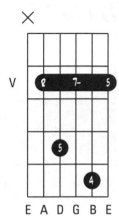

E A D G B E

In order to obtain a 7sus4 chord, raise the major 3rd of the 7th chord by one semitone (1 fret) so that it becomes the 4th. A 7sus4 chord does not include a 3rd: it is neither major nor minor.

D7sus4

Root = D; 4th = G; 5th = A; min 7th = C

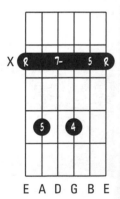

E A D G B E

If you have any difficulty in placing this chord, you need not play the lowest 5th (on the A string), as it can be found again on the B string.

Daug7 (7♯5, +7)

Root = D; maj 3rd = F♯; 5th♯ = A♯; min 7th = C

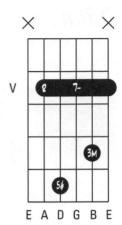

E A D G B E

An aug7 chord is a 7th chord in which the 5th has been raised by one semitone (1 fret). Please note that even if you press on the high E because of the barre chord, it should not be played.

Daug7 (7♯5, +7)

Root = D; maj 3rd = F♯; 5th♯ = A♯; min 7th = C

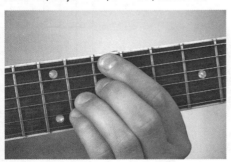

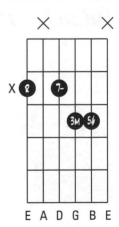

E A D G B E

An aug7 chord is a 7th chord in which the 5th has been raised by one semitone (1 fret).

Ddim7 (°7)

Root = D; min 3rd = F; 5thb = Ab; min 7th = Cb(B)

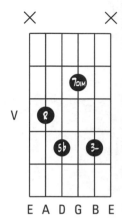

A dim7 chord is a 7th chord in which, with the exception of the root, all the notes have been lowered by one semitone (1 fret).

Ddim7 (°7)

Root = D; min 3rd = F; 5thb = Ab; min 7th = Cb(B)

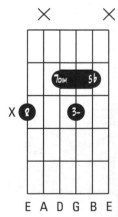

A dim7 chord is a 7th chord in which, with the exception of the root, all the notes have been lowered by one semitone (1 fret).

$Dmin^{M7}$ *(-M7, min△, -△)*

Root = D; min 3rd = F; 5th = A; maj 7th = C#

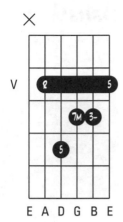

To obtain a min^{M7} chord, the minor 7th of the min7 chord must be augmented by one semitone (1 fret) so that it becomes major.

$Dmin^{M7}$ *(-M7, min△, -△)*

Root = D; min 3rd = F; 5th = A; maj 7th = C#

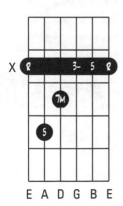

To obtain a min^{M7} chord, the minor 7th of the min7 chord must be augmented by one semitone (1 fret) so that it becomes major.

Dsus9

Root = D; 5th = A; 9th = E

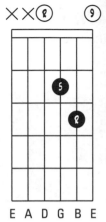

In order to obtain a sus9 chord, the major 3rd of the major chord must be lowered by two tones (2 frets) so that it becomes the 9th. A sus9 chord does not include a 3rd: it is neither major nor minor.

Dadd9

Root = D; maj 3rd = F#; 5th = A; 9th = E

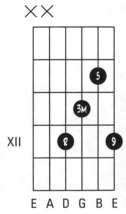

An add9 chord is a major chord to which a 9th has been added.

$D^{M7\ 9}$ *(Maj7 9, $\triangle$9)*

Root = D; maj 3rd = F$\sharp$; maj 7th = C$\sharp$; 9th = E

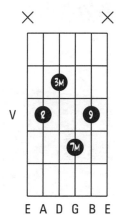

In order to play this form of $^{M7\ 9}$ chord on the guitar, we have removed the 5th of the ^{M7} chord situated on the D string so as to be able to place the 9th.

$D7^{9}$

Root = D; maj 3rd = F$\sharp$; maj 7th = C$\sharp$; 9th = E

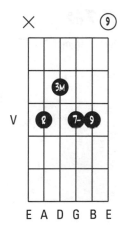

In order to play this form of 7^{9} chord on the guitar, we have removed the 5th of the 7th chord situated on the D string so as to be able to place the 9th.

D7$^{\flat 9}$

Root = D; maj 3rd = F$\sharp$; min 7th = C; 9$^{th}\flat$ = E$\flat$

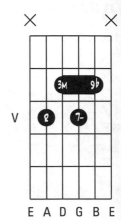

In order to play this form of 7$^{\flat 9}$ chord on the guitar, we have removed the 5th of the 7th chord situated on the D string so as to be able to place the 9$^{th}\flat$.

D7$^{\sharp 9}$

Root = D; maj 3rd = F$\sharp$; min 7th = C; 9$^{th}\sharp$ = E$\sharp$ (F)

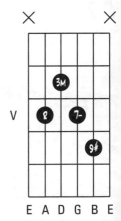

In order to play this form of 7$^{\sharp 9}$ chord on the guitar, we have removed the 5th of the 7th chord situated on the D string so as to be able to place the 9$^{th}\sharp$.

D7sus4^9

Root = D; 4th = G; 5th = A; min 7th = C; 9th = E

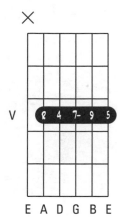

E A D G B E

In order to obtain a 7sus4^9 chord, raise the major 3rd of the 7^9 chord by one semitone (1 fret) so that it becomes the 4th. A 7sus4^9 chord does not include a 3rd: it is neither major nor minor.

Dmin7^9 *(m7^9, -7^9)*

Root = D; min 3rd F; min 7th = C; 9th = E

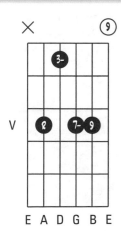

E A D G B E

In order to play this form of min7^9 chord on the guitar, we have removed the 5th of the min7 chord situated on the D string so as to be able to place the 9th.

$D^{M7\sharp11}$ (Maj7$\sharp$11, $\triangle\sharp$11)

Root = D; maj 3rd = F$\sharp$; maj 7th = C$\sharp$; 11th$\sharp$ = G$\sharp$

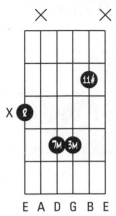

E A D G B E

In order to play this form of $^{M7}\sharp11$ chord on the guitar, we have removed the 5th of the ^{M7} chord situated on the B string so as to be able to place the 11$^{th}\sharp$.

$D7\sharp11$

Root = D; maj 3rd = F$\sharp$; min 7th = C; 11th$\sharp$ = G$\sharp$

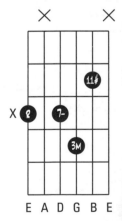

E A D G B E

In order to play this form of 7$^{\sharp11}$ chord on the guitar, we have removed the 5th of the 7th chord situated on the B string so as to be able to place the 11$^{th}\sharp$.

$Dmin7^{11}$ $(m7^{11}, -7^{11})$

Root = D; min 3rd = F; min 7th = C; 11th = G

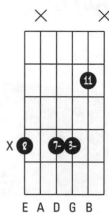

In order to play this form of min7[11] chord on the guitar, we have removed the 5th of the min7 chord situated on the B string so as to be able to place the perfect 11th.

$D^{M7\ 13}$ (Maj7 13, Δ 13)

Root = D; maj 3rd = F#; maj 7th = C#; maj 13th = B

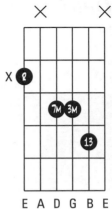

E A D G B E

In order to play this form of ^{M7} 13 chord on the guitar, we have removed the 5th of the ^{M7} chord situated on the B string so as to be able to place the major 13th.

$D7^{13}$

Root = D; maj 3rd = F#; min 7th = C; maj 13th = B

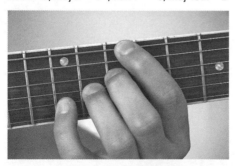

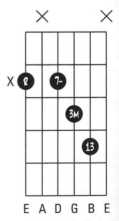

E A D G B E

In order to play this form of 7^{13} chord on the guitar, we have removed the 5th of the 7th chord situated on the B string so as to be able to place the major 13th.

D7^{b13}

Root = D; maj 3rd = F$\sharp$; min 7th = C; (min) 13th^b = B^b

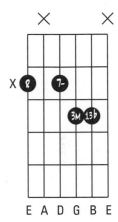

E A D G B E

In order to play this form of 7^{b13} chord on the guitar, we have removed the 5th of the 7th chord situated on the B string so as to be able to place the minor 13th (13th^b).

Part IV
E♭/D♯-family Chords

E♭/D♯ maj (M) *

Root = E♭; maj 3rd = G; 5th = B♭

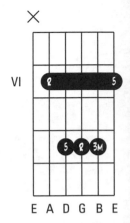

E♭/D♯ maj (M) *

Root = E♭; maj 3rd = G; 5th = B♭

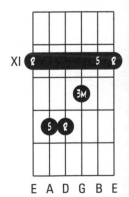

E♭/D♯ min (m, -)*

Root = E♭; min 3rd = G♭; 5th = B♭

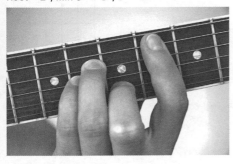

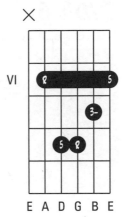

To obtain a minor chord, the major 3rd of the major chord must be lowered by one semitone (1 fret) so that it becomes minor.

E♭/D♯ min (m, -)*

Root = E♭; min 3rd = G♭; 5th = B♭

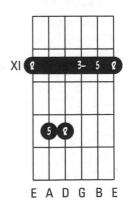

To obtain a minor chord, the major 3rd of the major chord must be lowered by one semitone (1 fret) so that it becomes minor.

E♭/D♯ 6

Root = E♭; maj 3ʳᵈ = G; maj 6ᵗʰ = C

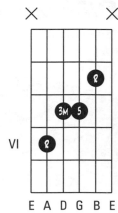

In order to play this form of 6ᵗʰ chord on the guitar, we have removed the 5ᵗʰ of the major chord so as to be able to place the major 6ᵗʰ.

E♭/D♯ 6

Root = E♭; maj 3ʳᵈ = G; 5ᵗʰ = B♭; maj 6ᵗʰ = C

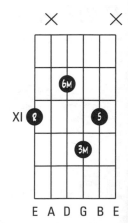

For this form of 6ᵗʰ chord on the guitar, we have lowered the root of the major chord situated on the D chord by one and a half tones (3 frets) so to obtain the major 6ᵗʰ.

E♭/D♯ min6 (m6, -6)

Root = E♭; min 3rd = G♭; 5th = B♭; maj 6th = C

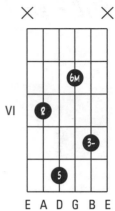

For this form of min6 chord on the guitar, we have lowered the root of the minor chord situated on the G chord by one and a half tones (3 frets) so to obtain the major 6th.

E♭/D♯ min6 (m6, -6) *

Root = E♭; min 3rd = G♭; 5th = B♭; maj 6th = C

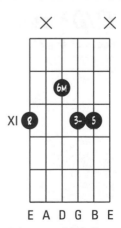

For this form of min6 chord on the guitar, we have lowered the root of the minor chord situated on the D chord by one and a half tones (3 frets) so to obtain the major 6th.

E♭/D♯ sus4

Root = E♭; 4th = A♭; 5th = B♭

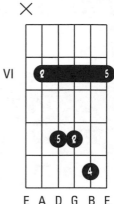

To obtain a sus4 chord, raise the 3rd of a major chord by one semitone (1 fret) so that it becomes the 4th. A sus4 chord does not include a 3rd: it is neither major nor minor.

E♭/D♯ sus4

Root = E♭; 4th = A♭; 5th = B♭

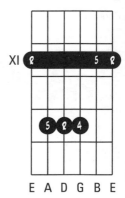

If you have any difficulty in placing this chord, you need not play the lowest 5th (on the A string), as it can be found again on the B string.

E♭/D♯ 5 *

Root = E♭; 5th = B♭

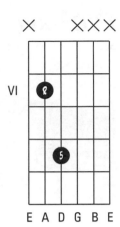

'5' chords consist of only 2 notes: the root and the 5th. Used a lot in rock and heavy metal, they are also referred to as *power chords*.

E♭/D♯ 5 *

Root = E♭; 5th = B♭

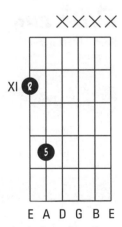

'5' chords consist of only 2 notes: the root and the 5th. Used a lot in rock and heavy metal, they are also referred to as *power chords*.

E♭/D♯ aug (♯5, +, 5+)

Root = E♭; maj 3rd = G; 5th♯ = B

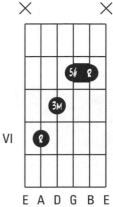

E A D G B E

An augmented chord is a major chord in which the 5th has been raised by one semitone (1 fret).

E♭/D♯ aug (♯5, +, 5+)

Root = E♭; maj 3rd = G; 5th♯ = B

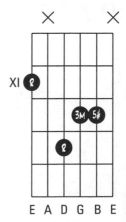

E A D G B E

If you have any difficulty in placing this chord, you need only play the 3 highest notes of the chord (the base note – in this case the root – may be omitted as it is repeated an octave higher).

E♭/D♯ dim (°)

Root = E♭; min 3rd = G♭; 5th♭ = B♭♭ (A)

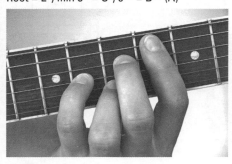

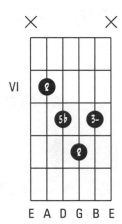

A diminished chord is a major chord in which, with the exception of the root, all the notes have been lowered by one semitone (1 fret).

E♭/D♯ dim (°)

Root = E♭; min 3rd = G♭; 5th♭ = B♭♭ (A)

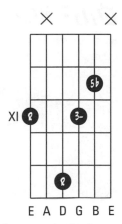

If you have any difficulty in placing this chord, you need only play the 3 highest notes of the chord (the base note – in this case the root – may be omitted as it is repeated an octave higher).

E♭/D♯ M7 (7M, Maj7, 7Maj, △)

Root = E♭; maj 3rd = G; 5thb = B♭; maj 7th = D

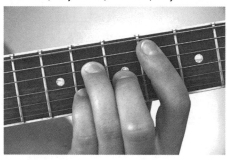

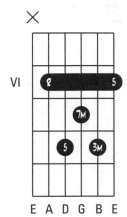

For this form of M7 chord on the guitar, we have lowered the root of the major chord situated on the G string by one semitone (1 fret) in order to obtain the major 7th.

E♭/D♯ M7 (7M, Maj7, 7Maj, △)

Root = E♭; maj 3rd = G; 5thb = B♭; maj 7th = D

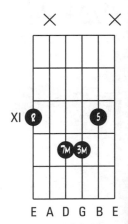

For this form of M7 chord on the guitar, we have lowered the root of the major chord situated on the D string by one semitone (1 fret) in order to obtain the major 7th.

E♭/D# 7 *

Root = E♭; maj 3rd = G; min 7th = D♭

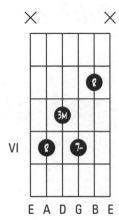

Please note that for this form of, currently used, 7th chord we have removed the 5th of the major chord on the G string so as to be able place the minor 7th.

E♭/D# 7

Root = E♭; maj 3rd = G; 5th = B♭; min 7th = D♭

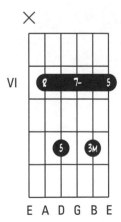

In order to obtain the 7th chord, the major 7th of the M7 chord must be lowered by one semitone (1 fret) so that it becomes minor.

E♭/D♯ 7

Root = E♭; maj 3ʳᵈ = G; 5ᵗʰ = B♭; min 7ᵗʰ = D♭

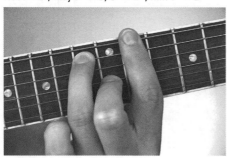
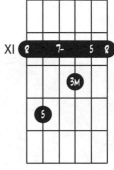

E A D G B E

In order to obtain the 7ᵗʰ chord, the major 7ᵗʰ of the ᴹ⁷ chord must be lowered by one semitone (1 fret) so that it becomes minor.

E♭/D♯ *min7* (m7, -7)

Root = E♭; min 3rd = G♭; 5th = B♭; min 7th = D♭

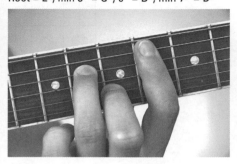

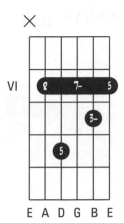

In order to obtain a min7 chord, the major 3rd of the 7th chord must be lowered by one semitone (1 fret) so that it becomes minor.

E♭/D♯ *min7* (m7, -7)

Root = E♭; min 3rd = G♭; 5th = B♭; min 7th = D♭

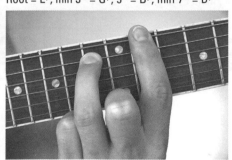

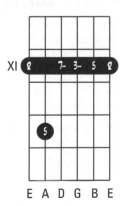

In order to obtain a min7 chord, the major 3rd of the 7th chord must be lowered by one semitone (1 fret) so that it becomes minor.

E♭/D♯ min7♭5 (m7♭5, -7♭5, ∅)

Root = E♭; min 3rd = G♭; 5th♭ = B♭♭ (A); min 7th = D♭

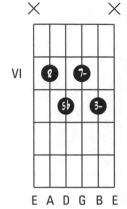

In order to obtain a min7♭5 chord, the 5th of the min7 chord must be lowered by one semitone (1 fret) so that it becomes a flat 5th (also known as a *diminished 5th*).

E♭/D♯ min7♭5 (m7♭5, -7♭5, ∅)

Root = E♭; min 3rd = G♭; 5th♭ = B♭♭ (A); min 7th = D♭

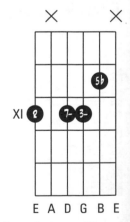

In order to obtain a min7♭5 chord, the 5th of the min7 chord must be lowered by one semitone (1 fret) so that it becomes a flat 5th (also known as a *diminished 5th*).

E♭/D♯ 7sus4

Root = E♭; 4th = A♭; 5th = B♭; min 7th = D♭

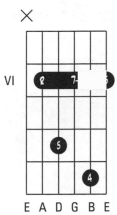

In order to obtain a 7sus4 chord, raise the major 3rd of the 7th chord by one semitone (1 fret) so that it becomes the 4th. A 7sus4 chord does not include a 3rd: it is neither major nor minor.

E♭/D♯ 7sus4

Root = E♭; 4th = A♭; 5th = B♭; min 7th = D♭

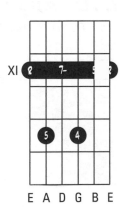

If you have any difficulty in placing this chord, you need not play the lowest 5th (on the A string), as it can be found again an octave higher.

E♭/D♯ aug7 (7#5, +7)

Root = E♭; maj 3rd = G; 5th# = B; min 7th = D♭

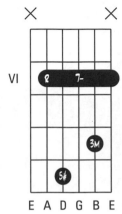

An aug7 chord is a 7th chord in which the 5th has been lowered by one semitone (1 fret). Please note that even if you press on the high E because of the barre chord, it should not be played.

E♭/D♯ aug7 (7#5, +7)

Root = E♭; maj 3rd = G; 5th# = B; min 7th = D♭

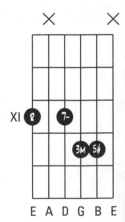

An aug7 chord is a 7th chord in which the 5th has been raised by one semitone (1 fret).

E♭/D♯ *dim7* (°7)

Root = E♭; min 3ʳᵈ = G; 5ᵗʰ♭ = B♭♭; dim 7ᵗʰ = D♭♭(C)

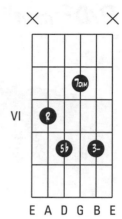

E A D G B E

A dim chord is a 7ᵗʰ chord in which, with the exception of the root, all the notes have been lowered by one semitone (1 fret).

E♭/D♯ *dim7* (°7)

Root = E♭; min 3ʳᵈ = G; 5ᵗʰ♭ = B♭♭; dim 7ᵗʰ = D♭♭(C)

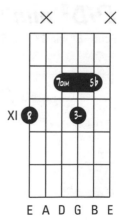

E A D G B E

A dim chord is a 7ᵗʰ chord in which, with the exception of the root, all the notes have been lowered by one semitone (1 fret).

E♭/D# min^M7 (-M7, min△, -△)

Root = E♭; min 3rd = G♭; 5th = B♭; maj 7th = D

×

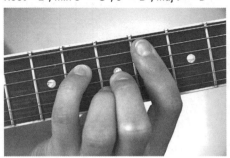

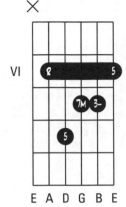

VI

E A D G B E

In order to obtain a min^M7 chord, the minor 7th of the min7 chord must be lowered by one semitone (1 fret) so that it becomes major.

E♭/D# min^M7 (-M7, min△, -△)

Root = E♭; min 3rd = G♭; 5th = B♭; maj 7th = D

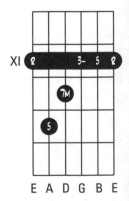

XI

E A D G B E

In order to obtain a min^M7 chord, the minor 7th of the min7 chord must be lowered by one semitone (1 fret) so that it becomes major.

E♭/D♯ sus9

Root = E♭; 5th = B♭; 9th = F

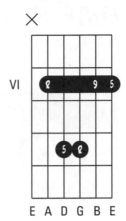

In order to obtain a sus9 chord, the major 3rd of the major chord must be lowered by one tone (2 frets) so that it becomes the 9th. A sus9 chord does not include a 3rd: it is neither major nor minor.

E♭/D♯ add9

Root = E♭; maj 3rd = G; 5th = B♭; 9th = F

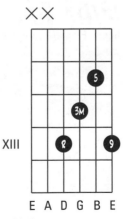

An add9 chord is a major chord to which a 9th has been added.

E♭/D♯ M7 9 (Maj7 9, Δ9)

Root = E♭; maj 3rd = G; maj 7th = D; 9th = F

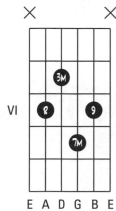

In order to play this form of M7 9 chord on the guitar, we have removed the 5th of the M7 chord situated on the D string so as to be able to place the 9th.

E♭/D♯ 7 9

Root = E♭; maj 3rd = G; min 7th = D♭; 9th = F

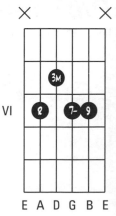

In order to play this form of 7 9 chord on the guitar, we have removed the 5th of the 7th chord situated on the D string so as to be able to place the 9th.

E♭/D♯ 7♭9

Root = E♭; maj 3rd = G; min 7th = D♭; 9th♭ = F♭ (E)

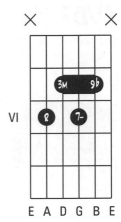

In order to play this form of 7 ♭9 chord on the guitar, we have removed the 5th of the 7th chord situated on the D string so as to be able to place the 9th♭.

E♭/D♯ 7♯9

Root = E♭; maj 3rd = G; min 7th = D♭ (B); 9th♯ = F♯

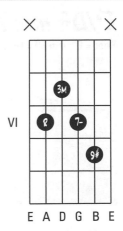

In order to play this form of 7 ♯9 chord on the guitar, we have removed the 5th of the 7th chord situated on the D string so as to be able to place the 9th♯.

E♭/D# 7sus4⁹

Root = E♭; 4th = A♭; 5th = B♭; min 7th = D♭; 9th = E♭

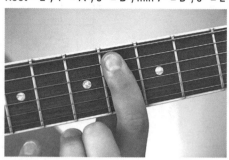

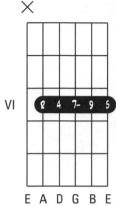

In order to obtain a 7sus4⁹ chord, raise the major 3rd of the 7⁹ chord by one semitone (1 fret) so that it becomes a 4th. A 7sus4⁹ chord does not include a 3rd: it is neither major nor minor.

E♭/D# min7⁹ (m7⁹, -7⁹)

Root = E♭; min 3rd = G♭; min 7th = D♭; 9th = F

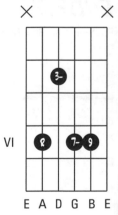

In order to play this form of min7⁹ chord on the guitar, we have removed the 5th of the min7 chord situated on the D string so as to be able to place the 9th.

E♭/D♯ M7♯11 (Maj7♯11, △♯11)

Root = E♭; maj 3rd = G; maj 7th = D; 11th♯ = A

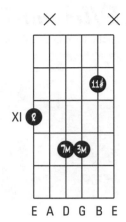

E A D G B E

In order to play this form of M7♯11 chord on the guitar, we have removed the 5th of the M7 chord situated on the B string so as to be able to place the 11th♯.

E♭/D♯ 7♯11

Root = E♭; maj 3rd = G; min 7th = D♭; 11th♯ = A

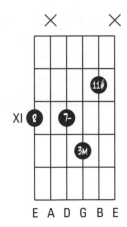

E A D G B E

In order to play this form of 7♯11 chord on the guitar, we have removed the 5th of the 7th chord situated on the B string so as to be able to place the 11th♯.

E♭/D♯ min7¹¹ (m7¹¹, -7¹¹)

Root = E♭; min 3ʳᵈ = G♭; min 7ᵗʰ = D♭; 11ᵗʰ = A♭

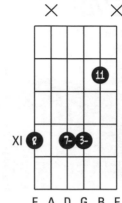

E A D G B E

In order to play this form of min7¹¹ chord on the guitar, we have removed the 5ᵗʰ of the min7 chord situated on the B string so as to be able to place the perfect 11ᵗʰ.

E♭/D♯ M7 13 *(Maj7 13, △ 13)*

Root = E♭; maj 3rd = G; maj 7th = D; maj 13th = C

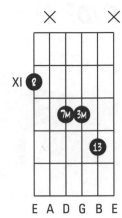

E A D G B E

In order to play this form of M7 13 chord on the guitar, we have removed the 5th of the M7 chord situated on the B string so as to be able to place the major 13th.

E♭/D♯ 7 13

Root = E♭; maj 3rd = G; min 7th = D♭; maj 13th = C

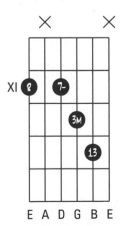

E A D G B E

In order to play this form of 7 13 chord on the guitar, we have removed the 5th of the 7th chord situated on the B string so as to be able to place the major 13th.

E♭/D# 7♭13

Root = E♭; maj 3rd = G; min 7th = D♭; (min) 13th♭ = C♭ (B)

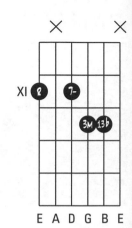

In order to play this form of 7♭13 chord on the guitar, we have removed the 5th of the 7th chord situated on the B string so as to be able to place the minor 13th (13th♭).

Part V
E-family Chords

Emaj (M) *

Root = E; maj 3rd = G#; 5th = B

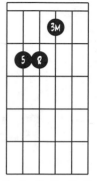

E A D G B E

Emaj (M) *

Root = E; maj 3rd = G#; 5th = B

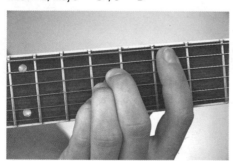

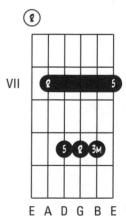

VII

E A D G B E

Emin (m, -) *

Root = E; min 3rd = G; 5th = B

In order to obtain a minor chord, the major 3rd of the major chord needs to be lowered by one semitone (1 fret) to make it minor.

Emin (m, -) *

Root = E; min 3rd = G; 5th = B

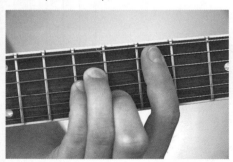

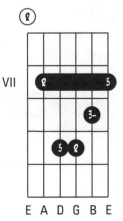

In order to obtain a minor chord, the major 3rd of the major chord needs to be lowered by one semitone (1 fret) to make it minor.

E6 *

Root = E; maj 3rd = G#; 5th = B; maj 6th = C#

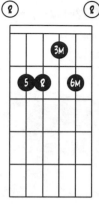

E A D G B E

For this form of 6th chord on the guitar, we have raised the 5th of the major chord situated on the B string by one tone (2 frets) in order to obtain the major 6th.

E6

Root = E; maj 3rd = G#; maj 6th = C#

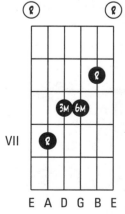

VII

E A D G B E

For this form of 6th chord on the guitar, we have removed the 5th of the major chord in order to place the major 6th.

Emin6 (m6, -6) *

Root = E; min 3rd = G; 5th = B; maj 6th = C$^{\sharp}$

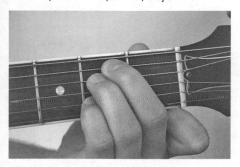

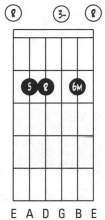

E A D G B E

For this form of 6th chord on the guitar, we have raised the 5th of the major chord situated on the B string by one tone (2 frets) in order to obtain the major 6th.

Emin6 (m6, -6)

Root = E; min 3rd = G; 5th = B; maj 6th = C$^{\sharp}$

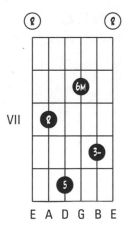

VII

E A D G B E

For this form of min6 chord on the guitar, we have lowered the root of the minor chord situated on the G string by one and a half tones (3 frets) in order to obtain the major 6th.

Esus4 *

Root = E; 4th = A; 5th = B

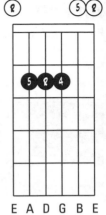

E A D G B E

In order to obtain a sus4 chord, raise the 3rd of a major chord by one semitone (1 fret) so that it becomes the 4th. A sus4 chord does not include a 3rd: it is neither major nor minor.

Esus4

Root = E; 4th = A; 5th = B

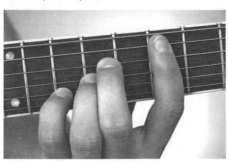

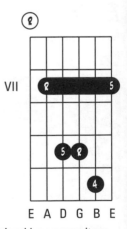

VII

E A D G B E

In order to obtain a sus4 chord, raise the 3rd of a major chord by one semitone (1 fret) so that it becomes the 4th. A sus4 chord does not include a 3rd: it is neither major nor minor.

E5 *

Root = E; 5th = B

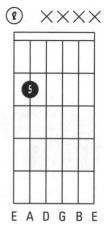

'5' chords consist of only 2 notes: the root and the 5th. Used a lot in rock and heavy metal, they are also referred to as *power chords*.

E5 *

Root = E; 5th = B

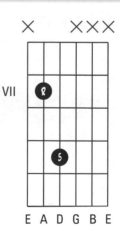

'5' chords consist of only 2 notes: the root and the 5th. Used a lot in rock and heavy metal, they are also referred to as *power chords*.

Eaug (♯5, +, 5+)

Root = E; maj 3rd = G♯; 5th♯ = B♯ (C)

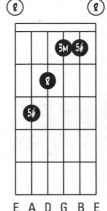

An augmented chord is a major chord in which the 5th has been raised by one semitone (1 fret).

Eaug (♯5, +, 5+)

Root = E; maj 3rd = G♯; 5th♯ = B♯ (C)

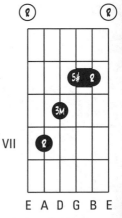

An augmented chord is a major chord in which the 5th has been raised by one semitone (1 fret).

Edim (°)

Root = E; min 3ʳᵈ = G; 5ᵗʰ♭ = B♭

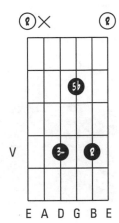

A diminished chord is a major chord in which, with the exception of the root, all the notes have been lowered by one semitone (1 fret).

Edim (°)

Root = E; min 3ʳᵈ = G; 5ᵗʰ♭ = B♭

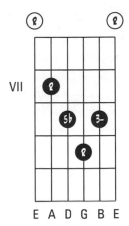

A diminished chord is a major chord in which, with the exception of the root, all the notes have been lowered by one semitone (1 fret).

E^{M7} (7M, Maj7, 7Maj, △) *

Root = E; maj 3rd = G#; 5th# = B; maj 7th = D#

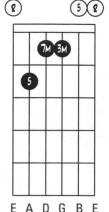

E A D G B E

For this form of M7 chord on the guitar, we have lowered the root of the major chord situated on the D string by one semitone (1 fret) in order to obtain the major 7th.

E^{M7} (7M, Maj7, 7Maj, △)

Root = E; maj 3rd = G#; 5th# = B; maj 7th = D#

VII

E A D G B E

For this form of M7 chord on the guitar, we have lowered the root of the major chord situated on the G string by one semitone (1 fret) in order to obtain the major 7th.

E7 *

Root = E; maj 3rd = G#; 5th = B; min 7th = D

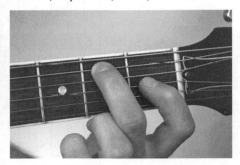

E A D G B E

In order to obtain the 7th chord, the major 7th of the M7 chord must be lowered by one semitone (1 fret) so that it becomes minor.

E7 *

Root = E; maj 3rd = G#; min 7th = D

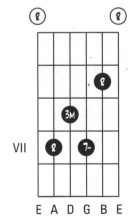

VII

E A D G B E

Please note that for this form of, currently used, 7th chord we have removed the 5th of the major chord so as to be able place the minor 7th.

E7

Root = E; maj 3rd = G#; 5th = B; min 7th = D

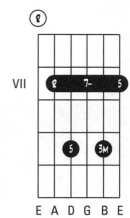

In order to obtain the 7th chord, the major 7th of the M7 chord must be lowered by one semitone (1 fret) so that it becomes minor.

Emin7 (m7, -7)

Root = E; min 3rd = G; 5th = B; min 7th = D

In order to obtain a min7 chord, the major 3rd of the 7th chord must be lowered by one semitone (1 fret) so that it becomes minor.

Emin7 (m7, -7)

Root = E; min 3rd = G; 5th = B; min 7th = D

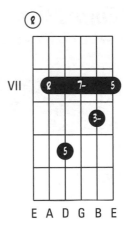

In order to obtain a min7 chord, the major 3rd of the 7th chord must be lowered by one semitone (1 fret) so that it becomes minor.

Emin7♭⁵ *(m7♭⁵, -7♭⁵, ø)*

Root = E; min 3rd = G; 5th♭ = B♭; min 7th = D

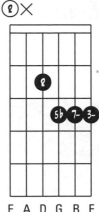

In order to obtain a min7♭⁵ chord, the 5th of the min7 chord must be lowered by one semitone (1 fret) so that it becomes a flat 5th (also known as a *diminished 5th*).

Emin7♭⁵ *(m7♭⁵, -7♭⁵, ø)*

Root = E; min 3rd = G; 5th♭ = B♭; min 7th = D

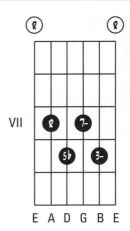

In order to obtain a min7♭⁵ chord, the 5th of the min7 chord must be lowered by one semitone (1 fret) so that it becomes a flat 5th (also known as a *diminished 5th*).

E7sus4

Root = E; 4th = A; 5th = B; min 7th = D

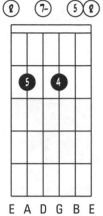

E A D G B E

In order to obtain a 7sus4 chord, raise the major 3rd of the 7th chord by one semitone (1 fret) so that it becomes the 4th. A 7sus4 chord does not include a 3rd: it is neither major nor minor.

E7sus4

Root = E; 4th = A; 5th = B; min 7th = D

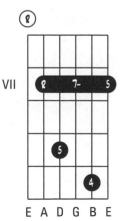

VII

E A D G B E

In order to obtain a 7sus4 chord, raise the major 3rd of the 7th chord by one semitone (1 fret) so that it becomes the 4th. A 7sus4 chord does not include a 3rd: it is neither major nor minor.

Eaug7 (7#5, +7)

Root = E; maj 3rd = G#; 5th = B# (C); min 7th = D

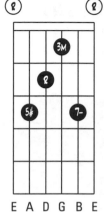

E A D G B E

An aug7 chord is a 7th chord in which the 5th has been raised by one semitone (1 fret).

Eaug7 (7#5, +7)

Root = E; maj 3rd = G#; 5th = B# (C); min 7th = D

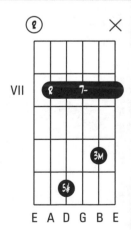

VII

E A D G B E

An aug7 chord is a 7th chord in which the 5th has been raised by one semitone (1 fret). Please note that even if you press on the high E because of the barre chord, it should not be played.

Edim7 *(°7)*

Root = E; min 3rd = G; 5^{th♭} = B♭; dim 7th = D♭

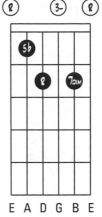

A dim7 chord is a 7th chord in which, with the exception of the root, all the notes have been lowered by one semitone (1 fret).

Edim7 *(°7)*

Root = E; min 3rd = G; 5^{th♭} = B♭; dim 7th = D♭

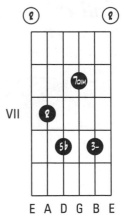

A dim7 chord is a 7th chord in which, with the exception of the root, all the notes have been lowered by one semitone (1 fret).

$Emin^{M7}$ *(-M7, min△, -△)*

Root = E; min 3rd = G; 5th = B; maj 7th = D#

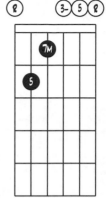

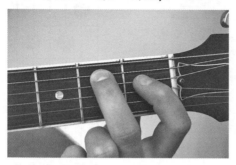

In order to obtain a min^M7 chord, the minor 7th of the min7 chord must be raised by one semitone (1 fret) so that it becomes major.

$Emin^{M7}$ *(-M7, min△, -△)*

Root = E; min 3rd = G; 5th = B; maj 7th = D#

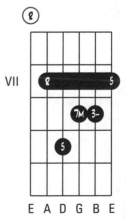

In order to obtain a min^M7 chord, the minor 7th of the min7 chord must be raised by one semitone (1 fret) so that it becomes major.

Esus9

Root = E; 5th = B; 9th = F[#]

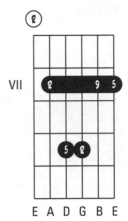

In order to obtain a sus9 chord, the major 3rd of the major chord must be lowered by one tone (2 frets) so that it becomes the 9th. A sus9 chord does not include a 3rd: it is neither major nor minor.

Eadd9 *

Root = E; maj 3rd = G[#]; 5th = B; 9th = F[#]

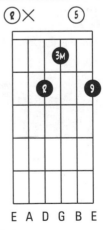

An add9 chord is a major chord to which a 9th has been added.

$E^{M7\ 9}$ *(Maj7 9, △9)*

Root = E; maj 3rd = G$\sharp$; maj 7th = D$\sharp$; 9th = F$\sharp$

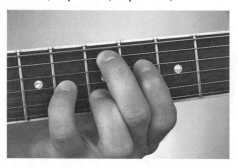

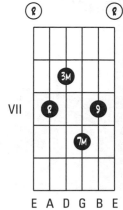

In order to play this form of $^{M7\ 9}$ chord on the guitar, we have removed the 5th of the ^{M7} chord situated on the D string so as to be able to place the 9th.

$E7\ ^9$

Root = E; maj 3rd = G$\sharp$; min 7th = D$\sharp$; 9th = F$\sharp$

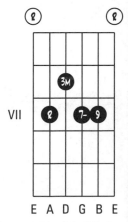

In order to play this form of 7^9 chord on the guitar, we have removed the 5th of the 7th chord situated on the D string so as to be able to place the 9th.

E7^{b9}

Root = E; maj 3rd = G$\sharp$; min 7th = D; 9th$\flat$ = F

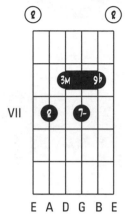

E A D G B E

In order to play this form of 7^{b9} chord on the guitar, we have removed the 5th of the 7th chord situated on the D string so as to be able to place the 9th$\flat$.

E7$^{\sharp9}$

Root = E; maj 3rd = G$\sharp$; min 7th = D; 9th$\sharp$ = F$\sharp\sharp$ (G)

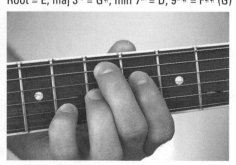

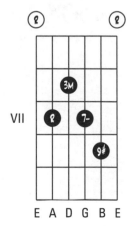

E A D G B E

In order to play this form of 7$^{\sharp9}$ chord on the guitar, we have removed the 5th of the 7th chord situated on the D string so as to be able to place the 9th$\sharp$.

E7sus4⁹

Root = E; 4th = A; 5th = B; min 7th = D; 9th = F#

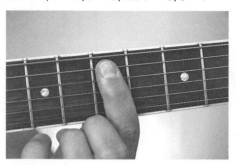

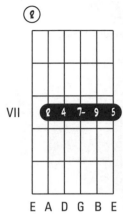

In order to obtain a 7sus4⁹ chord, raise the major 3rd of the 7⁹ chord by one semitone (1 fret) so that it becomes a 4th. A 7sus4⁹ chord does not include a 3rd: it is neither major nor minor.

Emin7⁹ (m7⁹, -7⁹)

Root = E; 4th = A; 5th = B; min 7th = D; 9th = F#

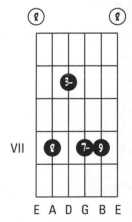

In order to play this form of min7⁹ chord on the guitar, we have removed the 5th of the min7 chord situated on the D string so as to be able to place the 9th.

$E^{M7\sharp11}$ *(Maj7#11, △ #11)*

Root = E; maj 3rd = G#; maj 7th = D#; 11th# = A#

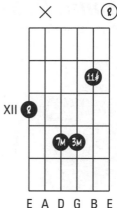

E A D G B E

In order to play this form of M7#11 chord on the guitar, we have removed the 5th of the M7 chord situated on the B string so as to be able to place the 11th#.

$E7^{\sharp11}$

Root = E; maj 3rd = G#; min 7th = D; 11th# = A#

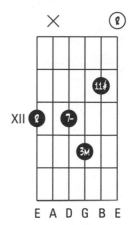

E A D G B E

In order to play this form of 7#11 chord on the guitar, we have removed the 5th of the 7th chord situated on the B string so as to be able to place the 11th#.

Emin7¹¹ (m7¹¹, -7¹¹)

Root = E; min 3rd = G; min 7th = D; 11th = A

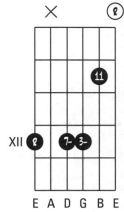

E A D G B E

In order to play this form of min7¹¹ chord on the guitar, we have removed the 5th of the min7 chord situated on the B string so as to be able to place the perfect 11th.

$E^{M7\ 13}$ *(Maj7 13, △ 13)*

Root = E; maj 3rd = G#; maj 7th = D#; maj 13th = C#

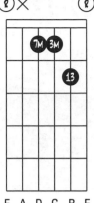

In order to play this form of M7 13 chord on the guitar, we have removed the 5th of the M7 chord situated on the B string so as to be able to place the major 13th.

E A D G B E

$E7^{\ 13}$

Root = E; maj 3rd = G#; min 7th = D; maj 13th = C#

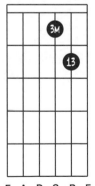

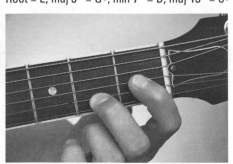

In order to play this form of 713 chord on the guitar, we have removed the 5th of the 7th chord situated on the B string so as to be able to place the major 13th.

E A D G B E

E7♭13

Root = E; maj 3ʳᵈ = G♯; min 7ᵗʰ = D; (min) 13ᵗʰ♭ = C

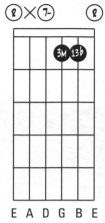

E A D G B E

In order to play this form of 7♭13 chord on the guitar, we have removed the 5ᵗʰ of the 7ᵗʰ chord situated on the B string so as to be able to place the minor 13ᵗʰ (13ᵗʰ♭).

Part VI
F-family Chords

Fmaj (M)*

Root = F; maj 3rd = A; 5th = C

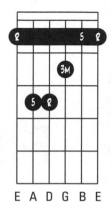

E A D G B E

Fmaj (M)*

Root = F; maj 3rd = A; 5th = C

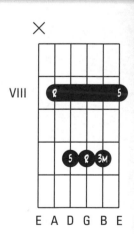

VIII

E A D G B E

Fmin *(m, -)* *

Root = F; min 3rd = A♭; 5th = C

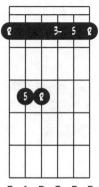

E A D G B E

In order to obtain a minor chord, the major 3rd of the major chord needs to be lowered by one semitone (1 fret) to make it minor.

Fmin *(m, -)* *

Root = F; min 3rd = A♭; 5th = C

×

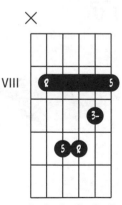

VIII

E A D G B E

In order to obtain a minor chord, the major 3rd of the major chord needs to be lowered by one semitone (1 fret) to make it minor.

F6

Root = F; maj 3rd = A; 5th = C; maj 6th = D

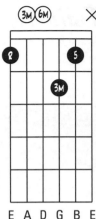

E A D G B E

For this form of 6th chord on the guitar, we have lowered the root of the major chord situated on the D string by one and a half tones (3 frets) in order to obtain the major 6th.

F6

Root = F; maj 3rd = A; maj 6th = D

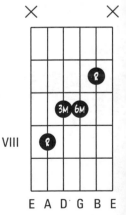

E A D G B E

In order to play this form of 6th chord on the guitar, we have removed the 5th of the major chord so as to be able to place the major 6th.

Fmin6 *(m6, -6)*

Root = F; min 3rd = A♭; 5th = C; maj 6th = D

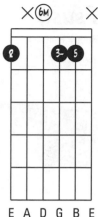

E A D G B E

For this form of min6 chord on the guitar, we have lowered the root of the minor chord situated on the D string by one and a half tones (3 frets) in order to obtain the major 6th.

Fmin6 *(m6, -6)*

Root = F; min 3rd = A♭; 5th = C; maj 6th = D

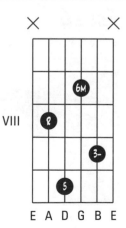

VIII

E A D G B E

For this form of min6 chord on the guitar, we have lowered the root of the minor chord situated on the G string by one and a half tones (3 frets) in order to obtain the major 6th.

Fsus4

Root = F; 4th = B♭; 5th = C

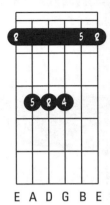

E A D G B E

TIP

If you have any difficulty in placing this chord, you can omit the lowest 5th (on the A string), as you can find it on the B string.

Fsus4

Root = F; 4th = B♭; 5th = C

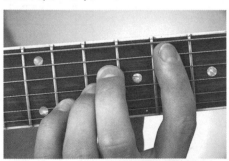

×

VIII

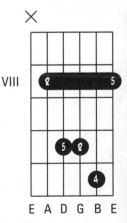

E A D G B E

In order to obtain a sus4 chord, raise the 3rd of a major chord by one semitone (1 fret) so that it becomes the 4th. A sus4 chord does not include a 3rd: it is neither major nor minor.

F5 *

Root = F; 5th = C

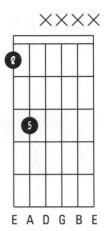

E A D G B E

'5' chords consist of only 2 notes: the root and the 5th. Used a lot in rock and heavy metal, they are also referred to as *power chords*.

F5 *

Root = C; 5th = G

VIII

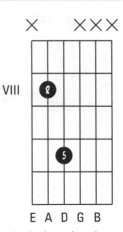

E A D G B

'5' chords consist of only 2 notes: the root and the 5th. Used a lot in rock and heavy metal, they are also referred to as *power chords*.

Faug (#5, +, 5+)

Root = F; maj 3rd = A; 5th# = C#

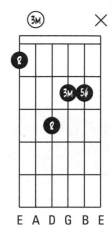

E A D G B E

TIP

If you have any difficulty in placing this chord, you need only play the 3 highest notes of the chord (the base note – in this case the root – may be omitted as it is repeated an octave higher).

Faug (#5, +, 5+)

Root = F; maj 3rd = A; 5th# = C#

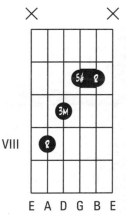

VIII

E A D G B E

An augmented chord is a major chord in which the 5th has been raised by one semitone (1 fret).

Fdim (°)

Root = F; min 3rd = A♭; 5th♭ = C♭ (B)

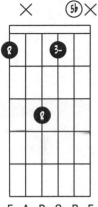

TIP

If you have any difficulty in placing this chord, you need only play the 3 highest notes of the chord (the base note – in this case the root – may be omitted as it is repeated an octave higher).

Fdim (°)

Root = F; min 3rd = A♭; 5th♭ = C♭ (B)

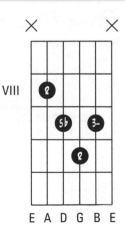

A diminished chord is a major chord in which, with the exception of the root, all the notes have been lowered by one semitone (1 fret).

F^{M7} (7M, Maj7, 7Maj, △) *

Root = F; maj 3rd = A; 5th = C; maj 7th = E

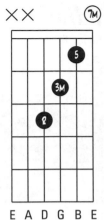

E A D G B E

For this form of ^{M7} chord on the guitar, we have lowered the root of the major chord situated on the high E string by one semitone (1 fret) in order to obtain the major 7th.

F^{M7} (7M, Maj7, 7Maj, △)

Root = F; maj 3rd = A; 5th = C; maj 7th = E

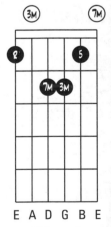

E A D G B E

For this form of ^{M7} chord on the guitar, we have lowered the root of the major chord situated on the D string by one semitone (1 fret) in order to obtain the major 7th.

F^{M7} (*7M, Maj7, 7Maj,* △) *

Root = F; maj 3rd = A; 5th = C; maj 7th = E

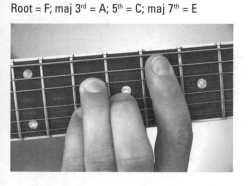

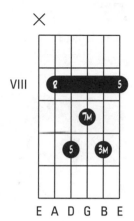

For this form of M7 chord on the guitar, we have lowered the root of the major chord situated on the G string by one semitone (1 fret) in order to obtain the major 7th.

F7

Root = F; maj 3rd = A; 5th = C; min 7th = E$^\flat$

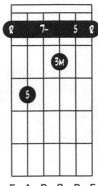

E A D G B E

In order to obtain the 7th chord, the major 7th of the ^{M7} chord must be lowered by one semitone (1 fret) so that it becomes minor.

F7 *

Root = F; maj 3rd = A; min 7th = E$^\flat$

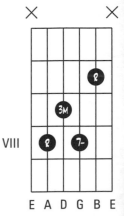

VIII

E A D G B E

Please note that for this form of, currently used, 7th chord we have removed the 5th of the major chord so as to be able place the minor 7th.

F7

Root = F; maj 3rd = A; 5th = C; min 7th = E$^\flat$

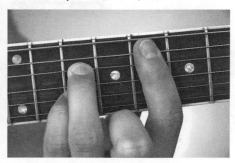

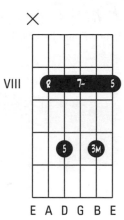

VIII

E A D G B E

In order to obtain the 7th chord, the major 7th of the ^{M7} chord must be lowered by one semitone (1 fret) so that it becomes minor.

Fmin7 (m7, -7)

Root = F; min 3rd = A♭; 5th = C; min 7th = E♭

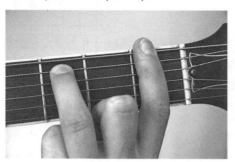

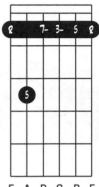

E A D G B E

In order to obtain a min7 chord, the major 3rd of the 7th chord must be lowered by one semitone (1 fret) so that it becomes minor.

Fmin7 (m7, -7)

Root = F; min 3rd = A♭; 5th = C; min 7th = E♭

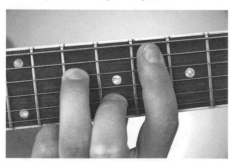

VIII

E A D G B E

In order to obtain a min7 chord, the major 3rd of the 7th chord must be lowered by one semitone (1 fret) so that it becomes minor.

Fmin7♭5 (m7♭5, -7♭5, ∅)

Root = F; min 3rd = A♭; 5th♭ = C♭ (B); min 7th = E♭

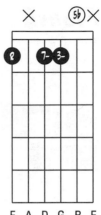

In order to obtain a min7♭5 chord, the 5th of the min7 chord must be lowered by one semitone (1 fret) so that it becomes a flat 5th (also known as a *diminished 5th*).

Fmin7♭5 (m7♭5, -7♭5, ∅)

Root = F; min 3rd = A♭; 5th♭ = C♭ (B); min 7th = E♭

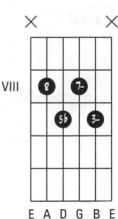

In order to obtain a min7♭5 chord, the 5th of the min7 chord must be lowered by one semitone (1 fret) so that it becomes a flat 5th (also known as a *diminished 5th*).

F7sus4

Root = F; 4th = B♭; 5th = C; min 7th = E♭

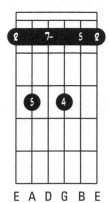

E A D G B E

If you have any difficulty in placing this chord, you need not play the lowest 5th (on the A string), as it can be found again on the B string.

F7sus4

Root = F; 4th = B♭; 5th = C; min 7th = E♭

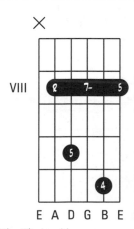

E A D G B E

In order to obtain a 7sus4 chord, raise the major 3rd of the 7th chord by one semitone (1 fret) so that it becomes the 4th. A 7sus4 chord does not include a 3rd: it is neither major nor minor.

Faug7 *(7$^{\sharp 5}$, +7)*

Root = F; maj 3rd = A; 5$^{th\sharp}$ = C$\sharp$; min 7th = E$\flat$

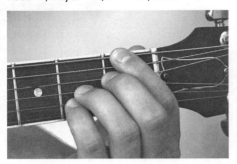

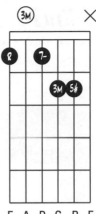

An aug7 chord is a 7th chord in which the 5th has been augmented by one semitone (1 fret).

Faug7 *(7$^{\sharp 5}$, +7)*

Root = F; maj 3rd = A; 5$^{th\sharp}$ = C$\sharp$; min 7th = E$\flat$

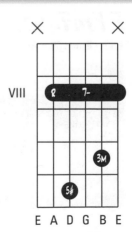

An aug7 chord is a 7th chord in which the 5th has been raised by one semitone (1 fret). Please note that even if you press on the high E because of the barre chord, it should not be played.

Fdim7 (°7)

Root = F; min 3rd = A$^\flat$; 5th$^\flat$ = C$^\flat$ (B); dim 7th = E$^{\flat\flat}$(D)

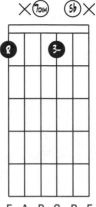

A dim7 chord is a 7th chord in which, with the exception of the root, all the notes have been lowered by one semitone (1 fret).

Fdim7 (°7)

Root = F; min 3rd = A$^\flat$; 5th$^\flat$ = C$^\flat$ (B); dim 7th = E$^{\flat\flat}$(D)

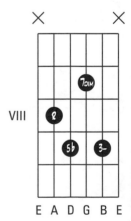

A dim7 chord is a 7th chord in which, with the exception of the root, all the notes have been lowered by one semitone (1 fret).

Fmin^M7 *(-M7, min^△, -△)*

Root = F; min 3rd = A♭; 5th = C; maj 7th = E

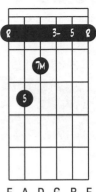

E A D G B E

In order to obtain a min^M7 chord, the minor 7th of the min7 chord must be raised by one semitone (1 fret) so that it becomes major.

Fmin^M7 *(-M7, min^△, -△)*

Root = F; min 3rd = A♭; 5th = C; maj 7th = E

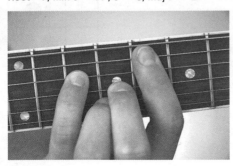

E A D G B E

In order to obtain a min^M7 chord, the minor 7th of the min7 chord must be raised by one semitone (1 fret) so that it becomes major.

Fsus9

Root = F; 5th = C; 9th = G

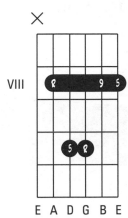

In order to obtain a sus9 chord, the major 3rd of the major chord must be lowered by one tone (2 frets) so that it becomes the 9th. A sus9 chord does not include a 3rd: it is neither major nor minor.

Fadd9

Root = F; maj 3rd = A; 5th = C; 9th = G

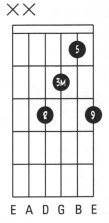

An add9 chord is a major chord to which a 9th has been added.

F$^{M7\ 9}$ (Maj7 9, Δ9)

Root = F; maj 3rd = A; maj 7th = E; 9th = G

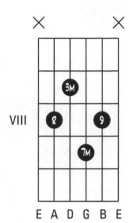

In order to play this form of $^{M7\ 9}$ chord on the guitar, we have removed the 5th of the ^{M7} chord situated on the D string so as to be able to place the 9th.

F7 ^{9}

Root = F; maj 3rd = A; maj 7th = E$^{\flat}$; 9th = G

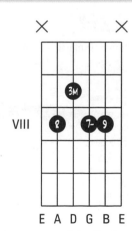

In order to play this form of 7 ^{9} chord on the guitar, we have removed the 5th of the 7th chord situated on the D string so as to be able to place the 9th.

F7♭9

Root = F; maj 3rd = A; min 7th = E♭; 9th♭ = G♭

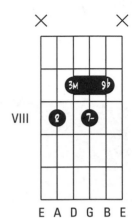

In order to play this form of 7 ♭9 chord on the guitar, we have removed the 5th of the 7th chord situated on the D string so as to be able to place the 9th♭.

F7♯9

Root = F; maj 3rd = A; min 7th = E♭; 9th♯ = G♯

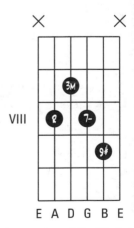

In order to play this form of 7 ♯9 chord on the guitar, we have removed the 5th of the 7th chord situated on the D string so as to be able to place the 9th♯.

F7sus4⁹

Root = F; 4th = B$^\flat$; 5th = C; min 7th = E$^\flat$; 9th = G

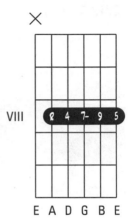

VIII

E A D G B E

In order to obtain a 7sus4⁹ chord, raise the major 3rd of the 7⁹ chord by one semitone (1 fret) so that it becomes the 4th. A 7sus4⁹ chord does not include a 3rd: it is neither major nor minor.

Fmin7⁹ *(m7⁹, -7⁹)*

Root = F; min 3rd = A$^\flat$; min 7th = E$^\flat$; 9th = G

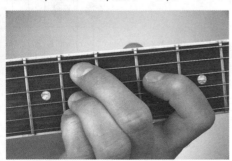

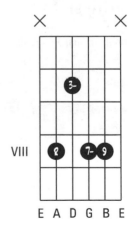

VIII

E A D G B E

In order to play this form of min7⁹ chord on the guitar, we have removed the 5th of the min7 chord situated on the D string so as to be able to place the 9th.

$F^{M7}\sharp^{11}$ *(Maj7#11, △ #11)*

Root = F; maj 3rd = A; maj 7th = E; 11th# = B

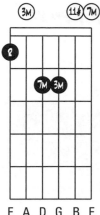

In order to play this form of $^{M7}\sharp^{11}$ chord on the guitar, we have removed the 5th of the ^{M7} chord situated on the B string so as to be able to place the 11th#.

$F7\sharp^{11}$

Root = F; maj 3rd = A; maj 7th = E; 11th# = B

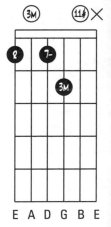

In order to play this form of $7^{\sharp11}$ chord on the guitar, we have removed the 5th of the 7th chord situated on the B string so as to be able to place the 11th#.

Fmin 7¹¹ *(m7¹¹, -7¹¹)*

Root = F; min 3rd = A♭; min 7th = E♭; 11th = B♭

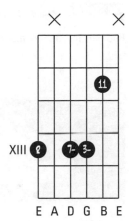

E A D G B E

In order to play this form of min7¹¹ chord on the guitar, we have removed the 5th of the min7 chord situated on the B string so as to be able to place the perfect 11th.

$F^{M7\ 13}$ *(Maj7 13, △ 13)*

Root = F; maj 3rd = A; maj 7th = E; maj 13th = D

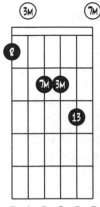

In order to play this form of $^{M7\ 13}$ chord on the guitar, we have removed the 5th of the ^{M7} chord situated on the B string so as to be able to place the major 13th.

$F7^{\ 13}$

Root = F; maj 3rd = A; min 7th = E♭; maj 13th = D

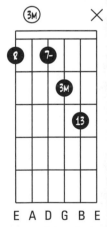

In order to play this form of 7^{13} chord on the guitar, we have removed the 5th of the 7th chord situated on the B string so as to be able to place the major 13th.

F7♭13

Root = F; maj 3rd = A; min 7th = E$^♭$; (min) 13$^{th♭}$ = D$^♭$

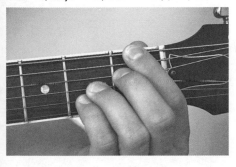

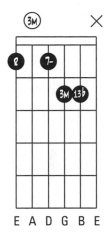

E A D G B E

In order to play this form of 7$^{♭13}$ chord on the guitar, we have removed the 5th of the 7th chord situated on the B string so as to be able to place the minor 13th (13$^{th♭}$).

Part VII
F#/G♭ Chords

F#/G♭ maj (M)*

Root = F#; maj 3rd = A#; 5th = C#

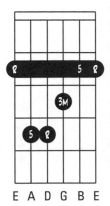

E A D G B E

F#/G♭ maj (M)*

Root = F#; maj 3rd = A#; 5th = C#

×

IX

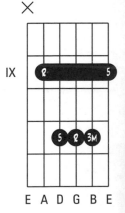

E A D G B E

F#/G♭ min (m, -)*

Root = F#; min 3rd = A; 5th = C#

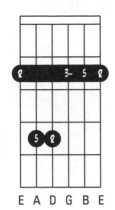

E A D G B E

In order to obtain a minor chord, the major 3rd of the major chord must be lowered by one semitone (1 fret) so that it becomes minor.

F#/G♭ min (m, -)*

Root = F#; min 3rd = A; 5th = C#

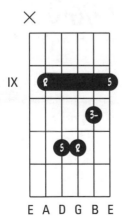

IX

E A D G B E

In order to obtain a minor chord, the major 3rd of the major chord must be lowered by one semitone (1 fret) so that it becomes minor.

F#/G♭6

Root = F#; maj 3rd = A#; 5th = C#; maj 6th = D#

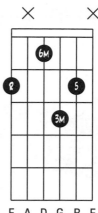

For this form of 6th chord on the guitar, we have lowered the root of the major chord situated on the D string by one and a half tones (3 frets) in order to obtain the major 6th.

F#/G♭6

Root = F#; maj 3rd = A#; maj 6th = D#

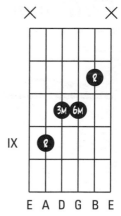

In order to play this form of 6th chord on the guitar, we have removed the 5th of the major chord in order to place the major 6th.

F#/Gb min6 *(m6, -6)*

Root = F# ; min 3rd = A ; 5th = C# ; maj 6th = D#

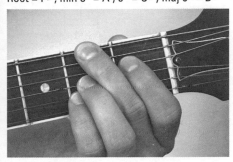

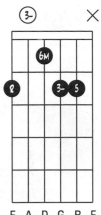

E A D G B E

For this type of min 6th chord on the guitar, we have lowered the root of the minor chord on the D string by a tone and a half (3 fret spaces) so as to get the major 6th.

F#/Gb min6 *(m6, -6)*

Root = F# ; min 3rd = A ; 5th = C# ; maj 6th = D#

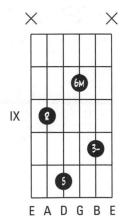

E A D G B E

For this type of min 6th chord on the guitar, we have lowered the root of the minor chord on the G string by a tone and a half (3 fret spaces) so as to get the major 6th.

F♯/G♭ sus4

Root = F♯ ; 4th = B ; 5th = C♯

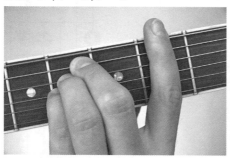

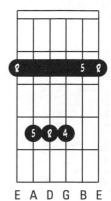

E A D G B E

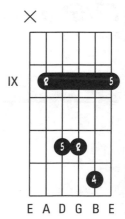

If you find it hard to place this chord, you can omit the lower-pitched 5th (on the A string), because you can find it on the B string.

F♯/G♭ sus4

Root = F♯ ; 4th = B ; 5th = C♯

×

IX

E A D G B E

To obtain an upper 4th chord, raise the 3rd of a major chord by a semitone (1 fret space), so that it becomes the 4th. A sus4th chord does not include the 3rd : it is not major or minor.

F♯/G♭ 5 *

Root = F♯ ; 5th = C♯

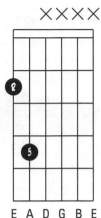

E A D G B E

'5' chords only have 2 notes: the root and the 5th. Widely used in rock and heavy metal, these are also called *power chords.*

F♯/G♭ 5 *

Root = F♯ ; 5th = C♯

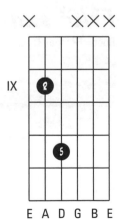

IX

E A D G B E

'5' chords only have 2 notes: the root and the 5th. Widely used in rock and heavy metal, these are also called *power chords.*

F#/Gb aug (#5, +, 5+)

Root = F# ; maj 3rd = A# ; 5th# = C## (D)

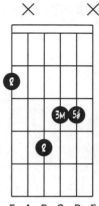

E A D G B E

TIP

If you find it hard to place this chord, you can just play the 3 highest notes of the chord (the bass – in this case the root – can be omitted because it is repeated one octave above)

F#/Gb aug (#5, +, 5+)

Root = F# ; maj 3rd = A# ; 5th# = C## (D)

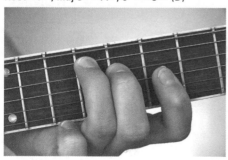

IX

E A D G B E

An augmented chord is a major chord where the 5th is raised a semitone (one fret space).

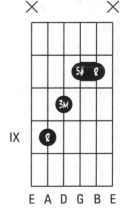

F#/G♭ dim (°)

Root = F# ; min 3rd = A ; 5th ♭ = C

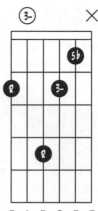

E A D G B E

TIP If you find it hard to place this chord, you can just play the 3 highest notes of the chord (the bass – in this case the root – can be omitted as it is repeated one octave above).

F#/G♭ dim (°)

Root = F# ; min 3rd = A ; 5th ♭ = C

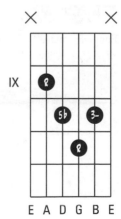

IX

E A D G B E

A diminished chord is a major chord where all the notes are lowered one semitone (1 fret space) except for the root.

F♯/G♭ M7 *(7M, Maj 7, 7Maj △)*

Root = F♯ ; maj 3rd = A♯ ; 5th = C♯ ; maj 7th = E♯ (F)

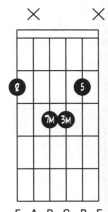

E A D G B E

F♯/G♭ M7 *(7M, Maj 7, 7Maj , △)*

Root = F♯ ; maj 3rd = A♯ ; 5th = C♯ ; maj 7th = E♯ (F)

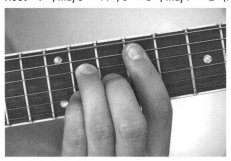

IX

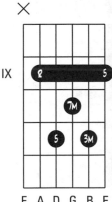

E A D G B E

For this type of M7 chord on the guitar, we have lowered the root of the major chord on the G string by a semitone (1 fret space) to obtain the major 7th.

F#/Gb 7

Root = F# ; maj 3 rd = A# ; 5th = C# ; min 7th = E

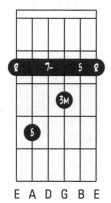

E A D G B E

To obtain a 7th chord, you must lower the major 7th of the M7 chord by one semitone so that it becomes minor

F#/Gb 7 *

Root = F# ; maj 3rd = A# ; min 7th = E

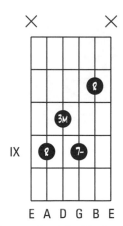

E A D G B E

Note that, for this type of frequently-used 7th chord, we have omitted the 5th of the chord to place the minor 7th.

F♯/G♭ 7

Root = F♯ ; maj 3 rd = A♯ ; 5th = C♯ ; min 7th = E

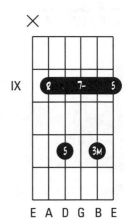

To obtain a 7th chord, you must lower the major 7th of the M7 chord by one semitone (1 fret space) to make it minor.

F#/G♭ min7 (m7, -7)

Root = F# ; min 3 rd = A ; 5th = C# ; min 7th = E

E A D G B E

To obtain a min7th chord, you must lower the major 3rd of the 7 chord by a
semitone (1 fret space) so that it becomes minor.

F#/G♭ min7 (m7, -7)

Root = F# ; min 3 rd = A ; 5th = C# ; min 7th = E

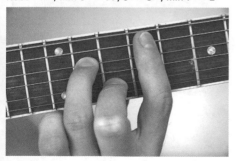

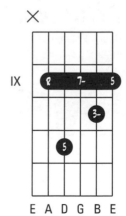

E A D G B E

To obtain a min7th chord, you must lower the major 3rd of the 7 chord by a
semitone (1 fret space) so that it becomes minor.

F#/G♭ min7♭5 (m7♭5, -7♭5, ∅)

Root = F# ; min 3rd = A ; 5th♭ = C ; min 7th = E

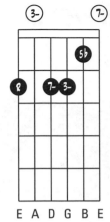

E A D G B E

To obtain a min 7♭5 chord, you must lower the 5th of the min7 chord by a semitone (1 fret space) so that it becomes a flattened 5th (also called *diminished 5th*).

F#/G♭ min7♭5 (m7♭5, -7♭5, ∅)

Root = F# ; min 3rd = A ; 5th♭ = C ; min 7th = E

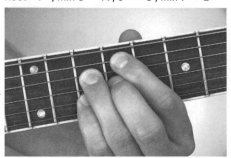

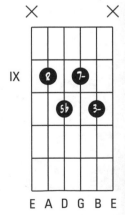

IX

E A D G B E

To obtain a min 7♭5 chord, you must lower the 5th of the min7 chord by a semitone (1 fret space) so that it becomes a flattened 5th (also called *diminished 5th*).

F#/G♭ 7sus4

Root = F# ; 4th = B ; 5th = C# ; min 7th = E

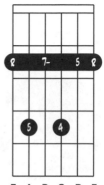

E A D G B E

TIP

If you find it hard to place this chord, you can omit the lowest 5th (on the A string), as you can find it on the B string.

F#/G♭ 7sus4

Root = F# ; 4th = B ; 5th = C# ; min 7th = E

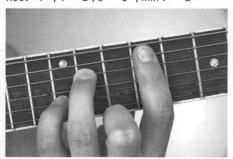

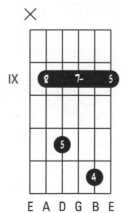

IX

E A D G B E

To obtain a 7th sus4th chord, raise the major 3rd of the 7th chord by a semitone (1 fret space) so that it becomes the 4th. A 7th sus4th chord has no 3rd : it is not major or minor.

F#/G♭ aug7 (7#5, +7)

Root = F# ; maj 3rd = A# ; 5th# = C## (D) ; min 7th = E

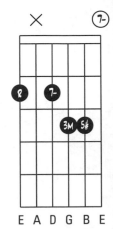

E A D G B E

An aug 7th chord is a 7th chord in which the 5th has been raised by a semitone (1 fret space).

F#/G♭ aug7 (7#5, +7)

Root = F# ; maj 3rd = A# ; 5th# = C## (D) ; min 7th = E

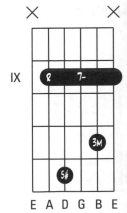

IX

E A D G B E

An aug 7th chord is a 7th chord in which the 5th has been raised by a semitone (1 fret space). Note that even if you press on the high E string because of the barre, you should not play it.

F#/G♭ dim 7 (°7)

Root = F# ; min 3rd = A ; 5th ♭ = C ; dim 7th = E♭

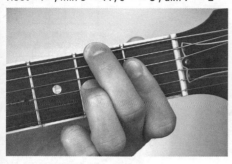

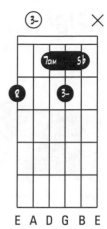

A dim 7th chord is a 7th chord in which all the notes have been lowered by a semitone (1 fret space) except for the root.

F#/G♭ dim 7 (°7)

Root = F# ; min 3rd = A ; 5th ♭ = C ; dim 7th = E♭

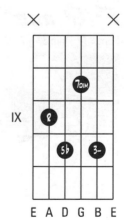

A dim 7th chord is a 7th chord in which all the notes have been lowered by a semitone (1 fret space) except for the root.

F♯/G♭ min^M7 (-M7, min △, -△)

Root = F♯ ; min 3rd = A; 5th = C♯ ; maj 7th = E♯ (F)

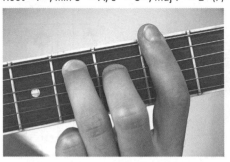

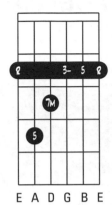

E A D G B E

To obtain a min ^M7 chord, you must raise the minor 7th of the min 7th chord by a semitone (1 fret space), so that it becomes major.

F♯/G♭ min^M7 (-M7, min △, -△)

Root = F♯ ; min 3rd = A; 5th = C♯ ; maj 7th = E♯ (F)

×

IX

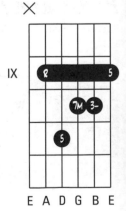

E A D G B E

To obtain a min ^M7 chord, you must raise the minor 7th of the min 7th chord by a semitone (1 fret space), so that it becomes major.

F#/Gb sus9

Root = F# ; 5th = C# ; 9th = G#

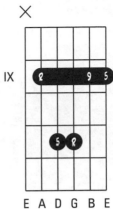

To obtain an extra 9th chord, you must lower the major 3rd of a major chord by a tone (2 fret spaces) so that it becomes the 9th. An extra 9th chord has no 3rd: it is not major or minor.

F#/Gb add9

Root = F# ; maj 3rd = A# ; 5th = C# ; 9th = G#

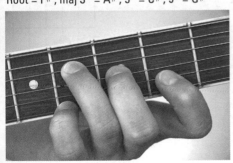

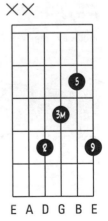

An add 9th chord is a major chord to which a 9th has been added.

F#/G♭ M7 9 *(Maj 7 9, ∆9)*

Root = F# ; maj 3rd = A# ; maj 7th = E# (F) ; 9th = G#

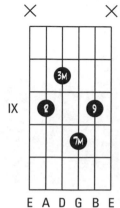

To play this type of chord on the guitar, we have removed the 5th from the M7 chord on the D string, so as to place the 9th.

F#/G♭ 7 9

Root = F# ; maj 3rd = A# ; min 7th = E ; 9th = G#

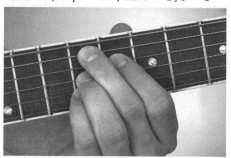

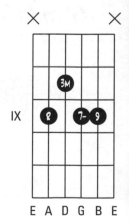

To play this type of 7 9 chord on the guitar, we have removed the 5th from the 7 chord on the D string, so as to place the 9th.

F#/Gb 7b9

Root = F# ; maj 3rd = A# ; min 7th = E ; b9th = G#

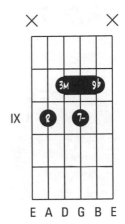

To play this type of 7 b9 chord on the guitar, we have removed the 5th from the 7 chord on the D string, so as to place the b9th.

F#/Gb 7#9

Root = F# ; maj 3rd = A# ; min 7th = E ; b9th = G#

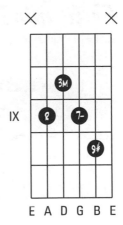

To play this type of 7 b9 chord on the guitar, we have removed the 5th from the 7 chord on the D string, so as to place the #9th.

F#/G♭ 7sus4⁹

Root = F# ; 4th = B ; 5th = C# ; min 7th = E ; 9th = G#

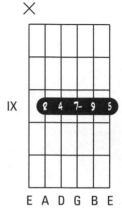

IX

E A D G B E

To obtain a 7th chord with extra 4⁹, raise the major 3rd of the 7th chord by one semitone (1 fret space) so that it becomes the 4th. A 7sus4⁹ chord has no third; it is not major or minor.

F#/G♭ min7⁹ (m7⁹, -7⁹)

Root = F# ; min 3rd = A ; min 7th = E ; 9th = G#

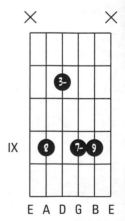

IX

E A D G B E

To play this type of minor 7th chord on the guitar, we have removed the 5th of the minor 7th chord on the D string so as to place the 9th.

F#/Gb M7#11 (Maj7#11, 6#11)

Root = F# ; maj 3rd = A# ; maj 7th = E# (F) ; 11th# = B# (C)

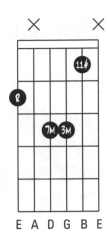

E A D G B E

To play this type of M7#11 chord on the guitar, we have removed the 5th of the M7 chord on the B string in order to place the 11th #.

F#/Gb 7#11

Root = F# ; maj 3rd = A# ; min 7th = E ; 11th# = B# (C)

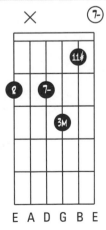

E A D G B E

To play this type of 7#11 cord on the guitar, we have removed the 5th from the 7th chord on the B string so as to place the 11th#.

F#/Gb min 7¹¹ (m7¹¹, -7¹¹)

Root = F# ; min 3rd = A ; min 7th = E ; 11th = B

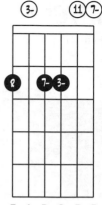

E A D G B E

To play this type of min 7¹¹ chord on the guitar, we have removed the 5th from the min 7 chord on the B string so as to place the perfect 11th.

F#/Gb M7 13 *(Maj7 13, △ 13)*

Root = F# ; maj 3rd = A# ; maj 7th = E# (F) ; maj 13th = D#

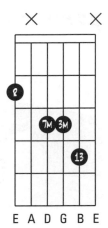

To play this type of M7 13 chord on the guitar, we have removed the 5th from the M7 chord on the B string so as to place the major 13th.

F#/Gb 7¹³

Root = F# ; maj 3rd = A# ; min 7th = E ; maj 13th = D#

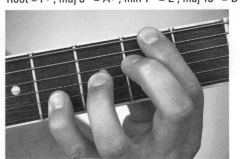

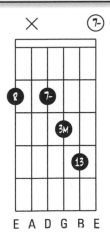

To play this type of 7¹³ chord on the guitar, we have removed the 5th from the 7th chord on the B string so as to place the major 13th.

F#/G♭ 7♭13

Root = F# ; maj 3rd = A# ; min 7th = E ; 13th♭ (min) = D

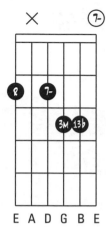

E A D G B E

To play this type of 7♭13 chord on the guitar, we have removed the 5th from the 7th chord on the B string so as to place the minor 13th (13♭)

Part VIII
G-family Chords

Gmaj (M)*

Root = G; maj 3rd = B; 5th = D

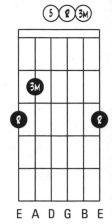

E A D G B E

Gmaj (M)*

Root = G; maj 3rd = B; 5th = D

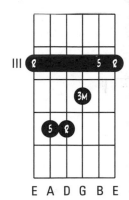

E A D G B E

Gmaj (M) *

Root = G; maj 3rd = B; 5th = D

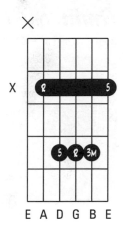

E A D G B E

Gmin (m, -) *

Root = G; min 3rd = B$^{\flat}$; 5th = D

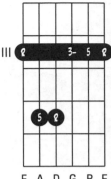

E A D G B E

To obtain a minor chord, lower the major 3rd of the major chord by a semitone (1 fret space) so that it becomes minor.

Gmin (m, -) *

Root = G; min 3rd = B$^{\flat}$; 5th = D

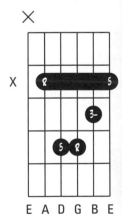

E A D G B E

To obtain a minor chord, lower the major 3rd of the major chord by a semitone (1 fret space) so that it becomes minor.

G6 *

Root = G; maj 3rd = B; 5th = D; maj 6th = E

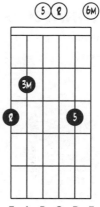

E A D G B E

For this type of 6th chord on the guitar, we have lowered the root of the major chord on the high E string by a tone and a half (3 fret spaces) to obtain the major 6th.

G6

Root = G; maj 3rd = B; maj 6th = E

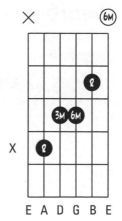

E A D G B E

To play this type of 6th chord on the guitar, we have removed the 5th from the major chord to as to place the major 6th.

Gmin6 (m6, -6)

Root = G; min 3rd = Bb; 5th = D; maj 6th = E

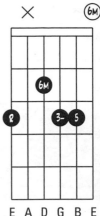

For this type of min6th chord on the guitar, we have lowered the root of the minor chord on the D string by a tone and a half (3 fret spaces) so as to obtain the major 6th.

Gmin6 (m6, -6)

Root = G; min 3rd = Bb; 5th = D; maj 6th = E

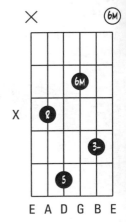

For this type of min6th chord on the guitar, we have lowered the root of the minor chord on the G string by a tone and a half (3 fret spaces) so as to obtain the major 6th.

Gsus4

Root = G; 4th = C; 5th = D

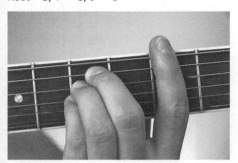

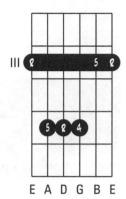

E A D G B E

TIP

If you find it hard to place this chord, you can omit the lowest 5th (on the A string), as you can find it on the B string.

Gsus4

Root = G; 4th = C; 5th = D

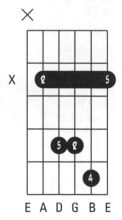

E A D G B E

To obtain a sus4 chord, raise the 3rd of a major chord by one semitone (1 fret space) so that it becomes the 4th. An extra 4 chord does not contain a 3rd : it is not major or minor.

G5 *

Root = G; 5th = D

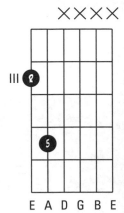

'5' chords only have 2 notes: the root and the 5th. Widely used in rock and heavy metal, these are also called *power chords*.

G5 *

Root = G; 5th = D

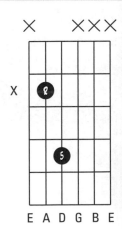

'5' chords only have 2 notes : the root and the 5th. Widely used in rock and heavy metal, these are also called *power chords*.

Gaug (#5, +, 5+)

Root = G; maj 3rd = B; 5th# = D#

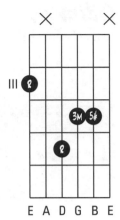

III

E A D G B E

TIP

If you find it hard to place this chord, you can just play the three highest notes of the chord. (The bass – in this case the root – can be omitted as it is repeated one octave above.)

Gaug (#5, +, 5+)

Root = G; maj 3rd = B; 5th# = D#

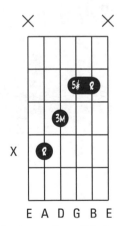

X

E A D G B E

An augmented chord is a major chord where the 5th is raised a semitone (1 fret space).

Gdim (°)

Root = G; min 3rd = B♭; 5th♭ = D♭

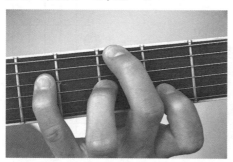

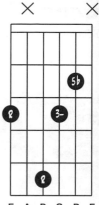

E A D G B E

If you find it hard to place this chord, you can just play the 3 highest notes of the chord. (The bass – in this case the root – can be omitted as it is repeated one octave above).

Gdim (°)

Root = G; min 3rd = B♭; 5th♭ = D♭

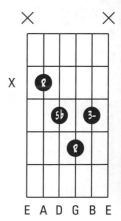

E A D G B E

A diminished chord is a major chord where all the notes are lowered by a semitone (1 fret space), except for the root.

G^{M7} *(7M, Maj7, 7Maj, △)* *

Root = G; maj 3rd = B; 5th = D; maj 7th = F$^\sharp$

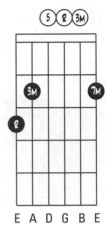

E A D G B E

For this type of chord on the guitar, we have lowered the root of the chord on the high E string by a semitone (1 fret space) to obtain the major 7th.

G^{M7} *(7M, Maj7, 7Maj, △)* *

Root = G; maj 3rd = B; 5th = D; maj 7th = F$^\sharp$

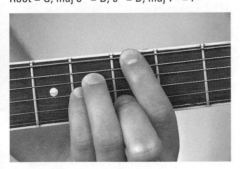

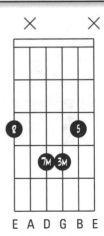

E A D G B E

For this type of chord on the guitar, we have lowered the root of the chord on the D string by a semitone (1 fret space) to obtain the major 7th.

G^{M7} *(7M, Maj7, 7Maj, $\triangle$)* *

Root = G; maj 3rd = B; 5th = D; maj 7th = F#

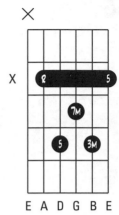

E A D G B E

For this type of chord on the guitar, we have lowered the root of the chord on the G string by a semitone (1 fret space) to obtain the major 7th.

G7 *

Root = G; maj 3rd = B; 5th = D; min 7th = F

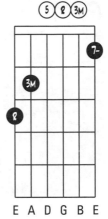

To obtain a 7th chord, lower the major 7th of the M7 chord by a semitone (1 fret space) so that it becomes minor.

G7

Root = G; maj 3rd = B; 5th = D; min 7th = F

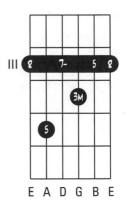

To obtain a 7th chord, lower the major 7th of the M7 chord by a semitone (1 fret space) so that it becomes minor.

G7 *

Root = G; maj 3rd = B; min 7th = F

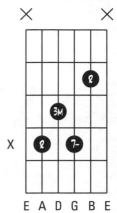

Note that, for this type of 7th chord, which is widely used, we have removed the 5th from the major chord so as to place the minor 7th.

G7

Root = G; maj 3rd = B; 5th = D; min 7th = F

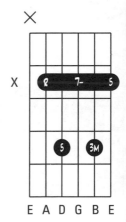

To obtain a 7th chord, lower the major 7th of the ^{M7} chord by a semitone (1 fret space) so that it becomes minor.

Gmin7 *(m7, -7)*

Root = G; min 3rd = Bb; 5th = D; min 7th = F

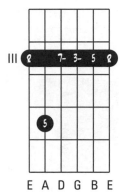

To obtain a minor 7th chord, lower the major 3rd of the 7th chord by a semitone (1 fret space) so that it becomes minor.

Gmin7 *(m7, -7)*

Root = G; min 3rd = Bb; 5th = D; min 7th = F

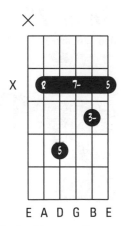

To obtain a minor 7th chord, lower the major 3rd of the 7th chord by a semitone (1 fret space) so that it becomes minor.

Gmin 7♭5 *(m7♭5, -7♭5, ∅)*

Root = G; min 3rd = B♭; 5th♭ = Db; min 7th = F

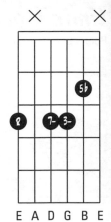

To obtain a min7♭5 chord, lower the 5th of the min7 chord by a semitone (1 fret space) so that it becomes a flattened 5th (also called a *diminished 5th*).

Gmin 7♭5 *(m7♭5, -7♭5, ∅)*

Root = G; min 3rd = B♭; 5th♭ = D♭; min 7th = F

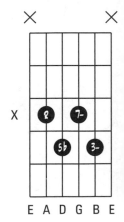

To obtain a min7♭5 chord, lower the 5th of the min7 chord by a semitone (1 fret space) so that it becomes a flattened 5th (also called a *diminished 5th*).

G7sus4

Root = G; 4th = C; 5th = D; min 7th = F

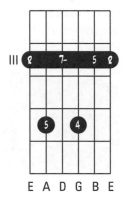

III

E A D G B E

If you find it hard to place this chord, you can omit the lowest 5th (on the A string), as you can find it on the B string.

G7sus4

Root = G; 4th = C; 5th =[D; min 7th = F

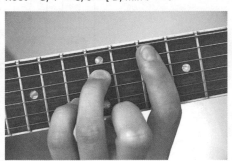

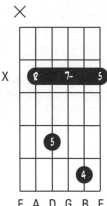

×

X

E A D G B E

To obtain a 7sus4 chord, raise the major 3rd of the 7 chord by a semitone (1 fret space) so that it becomes the 4th. A 7sus4 chord does not contain a 3rd : it is not major or minor.

Gaug7 *(7♯5, +7)*

Root = G; maj 3rd = B; 5th♯ = D♯; min 7th = F

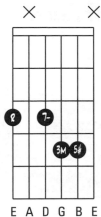

E A D G B E

An aug 7th chord is a 7th chord in which the 5th is raised by a semitone (1 fret space).

Gaug7 *(7♯5, +7)*

Root = G; maj 3rd = B; 5th♯ = D♯; min 7th = F

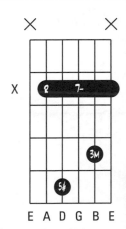

E A D G B E

An aug 7th chord is a 7th chord in which the 5th is raised by a semitone (1 fret space). Note that even if you press on the high E string because of the barre, you should not play it.

Gdim7 (°7)

Root = G; min 3rd = Bb; 5thb = Db; dim 7th = Fb (E)

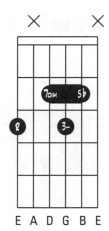

E A D G B E

A dim 7 chord is a 7th chord in which all the notes are lowered by a semitone (1 fret space) except for the root.

Gdim7 (°7)

Root = G; min 3rd = Bb; 5thb = Db; dim 7th = Fb (E)

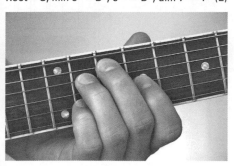

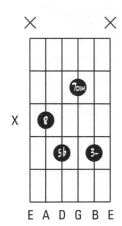

E A D G B E

A dim 7 chord is a 7th chord in which all the notes are lowered by a semitone (1 fret space) except for the root.

Gmin^{M7} (-*M7*, *min*△, -△)

Root = G; min 3rd = B♭; 5th = D; maj 7th = F♯

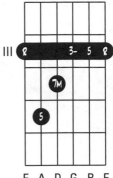

E A D G B E

To obtain a min^{M7} chord, raise the minor 7th of the min7 chord by a semitone (1 fret space) so that it becomes major.

Gmin^{M7} (-*M7*, *min*△, -△)

Root = G; min 3rd = B♭; 5th = D; maj 7th = F♯

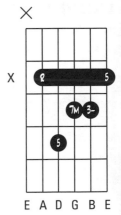

E A D G B E

To obtain a min^{M7} chord, raise the minor 7th of the min7 chord by a semitone (1 fret space) so that it becomes major.

Gsus9

Root = G; 5th = D; 9th = A

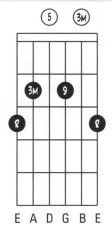

To obtain a sus9 chord, lower the major 3rd of the major chord by a tone (2 fret spaces) so that it becomes a 9th. A sus9 chord does not contain a 3rd: it is not major or minor.

Gadd9

Root = G; maj 3rd = B; 5th = D; 9th = A

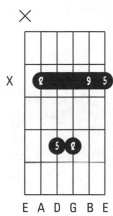

An add9 chord is a major chord with an added 9th.

$G^{M7\ 9}$ $(Maj7\ 9,\ \triangle 9)$

Root = G; maj 3rd = B; maj 7th = F#; 9th = A

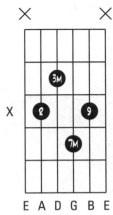

E A D G B E

To play this type of ^{M79} chord on the guitar, we have removed the 5th from the ^{M7} chord on the D string so as to place the 9th.

$G7^9$

Root = G; maj 3rd = B; min 7th = F; 9th = A

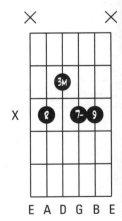

E A D G B E

To play this type of 7^9 chord on the guitar, we have removed the 5th from the 7th chord on the D string so as to place the 9th.

G7$^{♭9}$

Root = G; maj 3rd = B; min 7th = F; 9$^{th♭}$ = A$^♭$

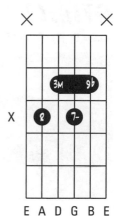

To play this type of 7$^{♭9}$ chord on the guitar, we have removed the 5th from the 7th chord on the D string so as to place the 9thb.

G7$^{♯9}$

Root = G; maj 3rd = B; min 7th = F; 9$^{th♯}$ = A$^♯$

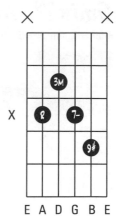

To play this type of 7$^{♯9}$ chord on the guitar, we have removed the 5th from the 7th chord on the D string so as to place the 9th♯.

G7sus4⁹

Root = G; 4th = C; 5th = D; min 7th = F; 9th = A

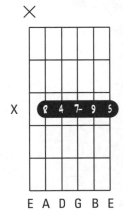

To obtain a 7sus4⁹ chord, raise the major 3rd of the 7⁹ chord by a semitone (1 fret space) so that it becomes the 4th. A 7sus4⁹ chord does not contain a 3rd : it is not major or minor.

Gmin7⁹ (m7⁹, -7⁹)

Root = G; min 3rd = B$^{\flat}$; min 7th = F; 9th = A

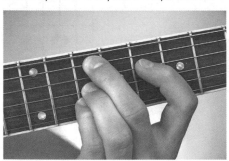

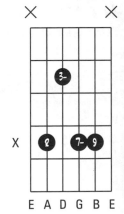

To play this type of min7⁹ chord on the guitar, we have removed the 5th from the min7th chord on the D string so as to place the 9th.

$G^{M7\sharp 11}$ (Maj7#11, △#11)

Root = G; maj 3rd = B; maj 7th = F#; 11th# = C#

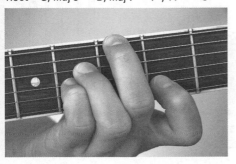

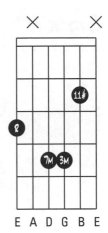

E A D G B E

To play this type of $^{M7\sharp 11}$ chord on the guitar, we have removed the 5th from the ^{M7} chord on the B string so as to place the 11th#.

$G7^{\sharp 11}$

Root = G; maj 3rd = B; min 7th = F; 11th# = C#

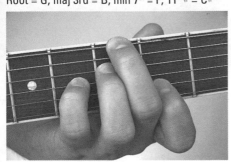

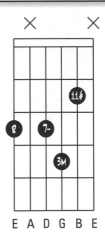

E A D G B E

To play this type of $7^{\sharp 11}$ chord on the guitar, we have removed the 5th from the 7th chord on the B string so as to place the 11th#.

Gmin7¹¹ *(m7¹¹, -7¹¹)*

Root = G; min 3rd = B♭; min 7th = F; 11th = C

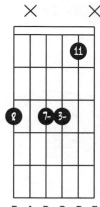

E A D G B E

To play this type of min7¹¹ chord on the guitar, we have removed the 5th from the min 7th chord on the B string so as to place the perfect 11th.

$G^{M7\ 13}$ *(Maj7 13, △ 13)*

Root = G; maj 3rd = B; maj 7th = F#; maj 13th = E

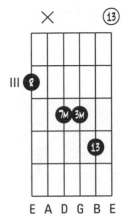

To play this type of M7 13 chord on the guitar, we have removed the 5th from the M7 chord on the B string so as to place the major 13th.

$G7^{13}$

Root = G; maj 3rd = B; min 7th = F; maj 13th = E

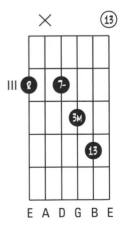

To play this type of 7¹³ chord on the guitar, we have removed the 5th from the 7th chord on the B string so as to place the major 13th.

G7 ♭13

Root = G; maj 3rd = B; min 7th = F; 13th♭ (min) = E♭

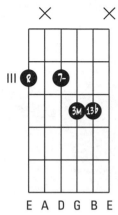

To play this type of 7♭13 chord on the guitar, we have removed the 5th from the 7th chord on the B string so as to place the minor 13th (13♭).

Part IX
A♭/G♯ Chords

A♭/G♯ maj (M) *

Root = A♭; maj 3ʳᵈ = C; 5ᵗʰ = E♭

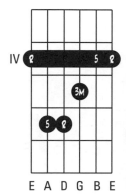

IV

E A D G B E

A♭/G♯ maj (M) *

Root = A♭; maj 3ʳᵈ = C; 5ᵗʰ = E♭

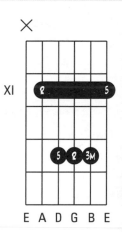

XI

E A D G B E

A♭/G♯ min (m, -) *

Root = A♭; min 3rd = C♭ (B); 5th = E♭

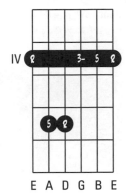

E A D G B E

To obtain a minor chord, lower the major 3rd of the major chord by a semitone (1 fret space) so that it becomes minor.

A♭/G♯ min (m, -) *

Root = A♭; min 3rd = C♭ (B); 5th = E♭

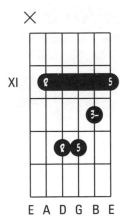

E A D G B E

To obtain a minor chord, lower the major 3rd of the major chord by a semitone (1 fret space) so that it becomes minor.

A♭/G♯6

Root = A♭; maj 3rd = C; 5th = E♭; maj 6th = F

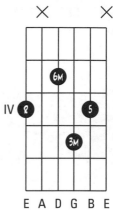

For this type of 6th chord on the guitar, we have lowered the root of the major chord on the D string by a tone and a half (3 fret spaces) to obtain the major 6th.

A♭/G♯6

Root = A♭; maj 3rd = C; maj 6th = F

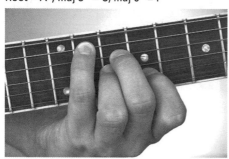

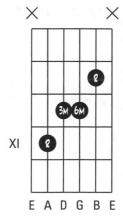

To play this type of 6th chord on the guitar, we have removed the 5th from the major chord so as to place the major 6th.

A♭/G♯ min6 (m6, -6)

Root = A♭; min 3rd = C♭ (B); 5th = E♭; maj 6th = F

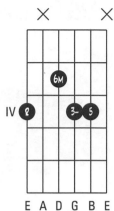

E A D G B E

For this type of min6 chord on the guitar, we have lowered the root of the minor chord on the D string by a tone and a half (3 fret spaces) so as to obtain the major 6th.

A♭/G♯ min6 (m6, -6)

Root = A♭; min 3rd = C♭ (B); 5th = E♭; maj 6th = F

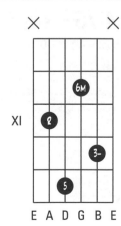

E A D G B E

For this type of min6 chord on the guitar, we have lowered the root of the minor chord on the G string by a tone and a half (3 fret spaces) so as to obtain the major 6th.

A♭/G♯ sus4

Root = A♭; 4th = D♭; 5th = E♭

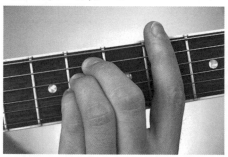

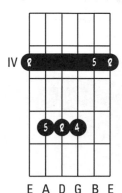

IV

E A D G B E

TIP

If you find it hard to place this chord, you can omit the lowest 5th (on the A string) as you can find it on the B string.

A♭/G♯ sus4

Root = A♭; 4th = D♭; 5th = E♭

×

XI

E A D G B E

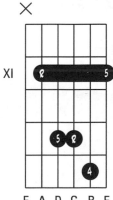

To obtain a sus4 chord, raise the 3rd of a major chord by a semitone (1 fret space) so that it becomes the 4th. An extra 4 chord has no 3rd : it is not major or minor.

A♭/G♯ 5 *

Root = A♭; 5th = E♭

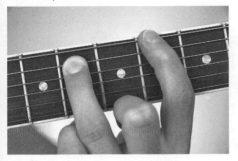

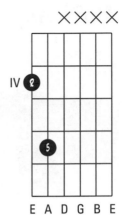

××××

IV

'5' chords only have 2 notes: the root and the 5th. Widely used in rock and heavy metal, they are also called *power chords*.

A♭/G♯ 5 *

Root = A♭; 5th = E♭

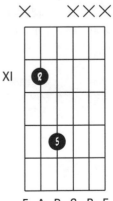

× ×××

XI

'5' chords only have 2 notes: the root and the 5th. Widely used in rock and heavy metal, they are also called *power chords*.

A♭/G♯ aug (♯5, +, 5+)

Root = A♭; maj 3rd = C; 5th♯ = E

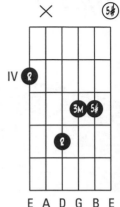

TIP

If you find it hard to place this chord, you can just play the 3 highest notes of the chord. (the bass – in this case the root – can be omitted as it is repeated one octave above).

A♭/G♯ aug (♯5, +, 5+)

Root = A♭; maj 3rd = C; 5th♯ = E

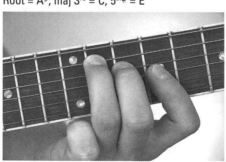

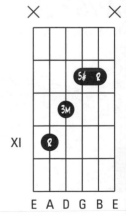

An augmented chord is a major chord in which the 5th is raised by a semitone (1 fret space).

A♭/G♯ dim (°)

Root = A♭; min 3ʳᵈ = C♭ (B); 5ᵗʰ♭ = E♭♭ (D)

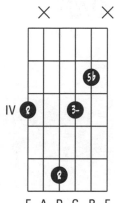

E A D G B E

If you find it hard to place this chord, you can just play the 3 highest notes of the chord. (the bass – in this case the root – can be omitted as it is repeated one octave above).

A♭/G♯ dim (°)

Root = A♭; min 3ʳᵈ = C♭ (B); 5ᵗʰ♭ = E♭♭ (D)

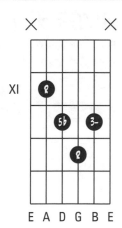

E A D G B E

A diminished chord is a major chord in which all the notes are lowered by a semitone (1 fret space), except for the root.

A♭/G♯ M7 *(7M, Maj7, 7Maj, △)*

Root = A♭; maj 3ʳᵈ: C; 5ᵗʰ = E♭; maj 7ᵗʰ = G

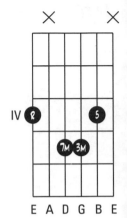

IV

E A D G B E

For this type of ᴹ⁷ chord on the guitar, we have lowered the root of the major chord on the D string by a semitone (1 fret space), to obtain the major 7ᵗʰ.

A♭/G♯ M7 *(7M, Maj7, 7Maj, △)*

Root = A♭; maj 3ʳᵈ: C; 5ᵗʰ = E♭; maj 7ᵗʰ = G

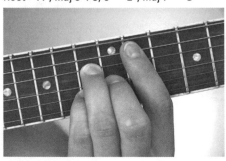

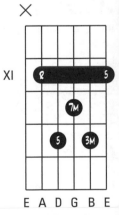

XI

E A D G B E

For this type of ᴹ⁷ chord on the guitar, we have lowered the root of the major chord on the G string by a semitone (1 fret space), to obtain the major 7ᵗʰ.

A♭/G♯ 7 *

Root = A♭; maj 3ʳᵈ: C; 5ᵗʰ = E♭; min 7ᵗʰ = =G♭

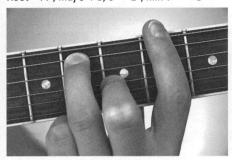

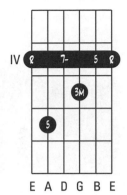

For this type of ᴹ⁷ chord on the guitar, lower the major 7ᵗʰ of the M7 chord by a semitone (1 fret space) so that this becomes minor.

A♭/G♯ 7 *

Root = A♭; maj 3ʳᵈ: C; min 7ᵗʰ = =G♭

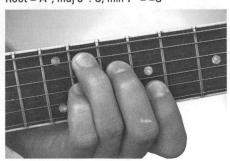

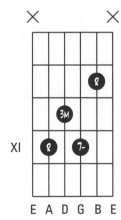

Note that for this type of 7th chord, which is widely used, we have removed the 5ᵗʰ of the major chord in order to place the minor 7ᵗʰ.

A♭/G♯ 7

Root = A♭; maj 3rd = C; 5th = E♭; min 7th = G♭

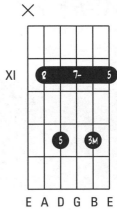

E A D G B E

To obtain a 7th chord, lower the major 7th of the M7 chord by a semitone (1 fret space) so that it becomes minor.

A♭/G♯ *min7 (m7, -7)*

Root = A♭; min 3rd = C♭ (B); 5th = E♭; min 7th = G♭

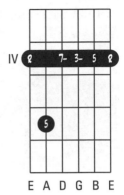

IV

E A D G B E

To obtain a min 7th chord, lower the major 3rd of the 7th chord by a semitone (1 fret space) so that this becomes minor.

A♭/G♯ *min7 (m7, -7)*

Root = A♭; min 3rd = C♭ (B); 5th = E♭; min 7th = G♭

×

XI

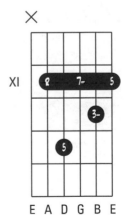

E A D G B E

To obtain a min 7th chord, lower the major 3rd of the 7th chord by a semitone (1 fret space) so that this becomes minor.

A♭/G♯ *min7♭5* (*m7♭5, -7♭5, ∅*)

Root = A♭; min 3rd = C♭; 5th♭; E♭♭(D); min 7th = G♭

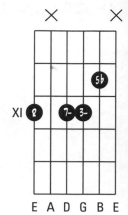

To obtain a min7♭5 chord, lower the 5th of the min7 chord by a semitone (1 fret space) so that this becomes a flat 5th (also called *diminished 5th*).

A♭/G♯ *min7♭5* (*m7♭5, -7♭5, ∅*)

Root = A♭; min 3rd = C♭; 5th♭; E♭♭(D); min 7th = G♭

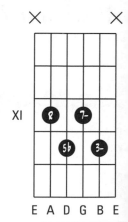

To obtain a min7♭5 chord, lower the 5th of the min7 chord by a semitone (1 fret space) so that this becomes a flat 5th (also called *diminished 5th*).

A♭/G♯ 7sus4

Root = A♭; 4th = D♭; 5th = E♭; min 7th = G♭

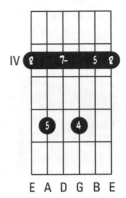

TIP

If you find it hard to place this chord, you can omit the lowest 5th (on the A string), as you can find this on the B string.

A♭/G♯ 7sus4

Root = A♭; 4th = D♭; 5th = E♭; min 7th = G♭

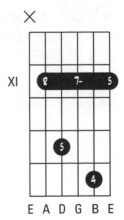

To obtain a 7sus4 chord, raise the major 3rd of the 7th chord by a semitone (1 fret space) so that it becomes the 4th. A 7sus4 chord has no 3rd: it is not major or minor.

A♭/G♯ aug7 (7♯5, +7)

Root = A♭; Maj 3rd = C; 5th♯ = E; min 7th = G♭

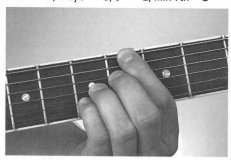

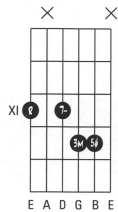

XI

E A D G B E

An aug7 chord is a 7th chord in which the 5th is raised by a semitone (1 fret space).

A♭/G♯ aug7 (7♯5, +7)

Root = A♭; Maj 3rd = C; 5th♯ = E; min 7th = G♭

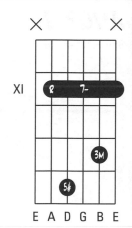

XI

E A D G B E

An aug7 chord is a 7th chord in which the 5th is raised by a semitone (1 fret space). Note that even if you press on the high E string because of the barre, you should not play it.

A♭/G♯ dim7 (°7)

Root = A♭; min 3rd = C♭ (B); 5th♭ = E♭ ♭(D); dim 7th = G♭ ♭ (F)

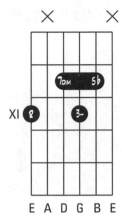

A dim7 chord is a 7th chord in which all the notes are lowered by a semitone (1 fret space) except for the root.

A♭/G♯ dim7 (°7)

Root = A♭; min 3rd = C♭ (B); 5th♭ = E♭ ♭ (D); dim 7th = G♭ ♭ (F)

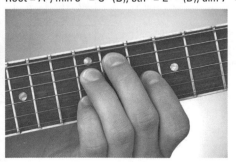

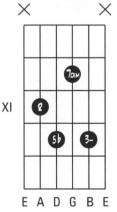

A dim7 chord is a 7th chord in which all the notes are lowered by a semitone (1 fret space) except for the root.

A♭/G♯ min^M7 (-M7, min△, -△)

Root = A♭; min 3rd = C♭ (B); 5th = E♭; maj 7th = G

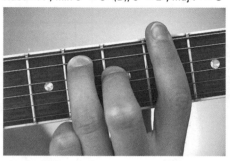

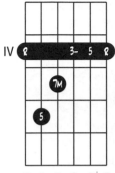

To obtain a min^M7 chord, raise the minor 7th of the min7 chord by a semitone (1 fret space) so that it becomes major.

A♭/G♯ min^M7 (-M7, min△, -△)

Root = A♭; min 3rd = C♭ (B); 5th = E♭; maj 7th = G

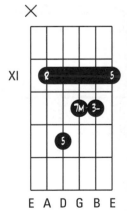

To obtain a min^M7 chord, raise the minor 7th of the min7 chord by a semitone (1 fret space) so that it becomes major.

A♭/G♯ sus9

Root = A♭; 5th = E♭; 9th = B♭

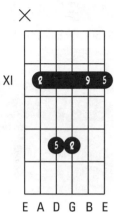

To obtain a sus9 chord, lower the major 3rd of the major chord by a tone (2 fret spaces), so that it becomes the 9th. A sus9 chord had no 3rd: it is not major or minor.

A♭/G♯ add9

Root = A♭; maj 3rd = C; 5th = E♭; 9th = B♭

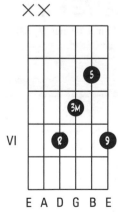

An add9 chord is a major chord with an added 9th.

A♭/G♯ M7 9 (Maj7 9, Δ9)

Root = A♭; maj 3rd = C; maj 7th = G; 9th = B♭

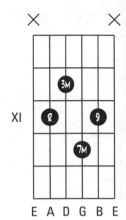

To play this type of M7 9 chord on the guitar, we have removed the 5th of the M7 chord on the D string, in order to place the 9th.

A♭/G♯ 7⁹

Root = A♭; maj 3rd = C; min 7th = G♭; 9th = B♭

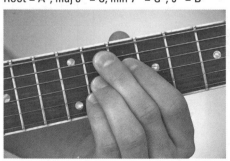

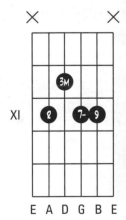

To play this type of 7⁹ chord on the guitar, we have removed the 5th of the 7th chord on the D string, in order to place the 9th.

A♭/G♯ 7♭9

Root = A♭; maj 3rd = C; min 7th = G♭; 9thb = B♭♭ (A)

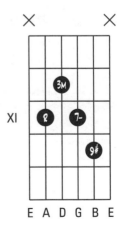

To play this type of 7♭9 chord on the guitar, we have removed the 5th of the 7th chord on the D string, in order to place the 9thb.

A♭/G♯ 7♯9

Root = A♭; maj 3rd = C; min 7th = G♭; 9th♯ = B

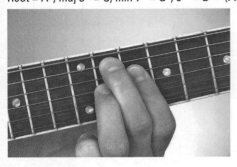

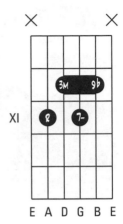

To play this type of 7♯9 chord on the guitar, we have removed the 5th of the 7th chord on the D string, in order to place the 9th♯.

A♭/G♯ 7sus4⁹

Root = A♭; 4th = D♭; 5th = E♭; min 7th = G♭; 9th = B♭

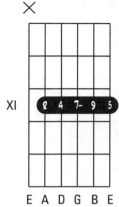

XI

E A D G B E

To obtain a 7sus4⁹, raise the major 3rd of the 7⁹ chord by a semitone (1 fret space), so that it becomes the 4th. A 7sus4⁹ chord has no 3rd: it is not major or minor.

A♭/G♯ min7⁹ (m7⁹, -7⁹)

Root = A♭; min 3rd = C♭ (B); min 7th = G♭; 9th = B♭

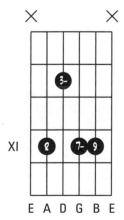

XI

E A D G B E

To play this type of min7⁹ chord on the guitar, we have removed the 5th from the min7 chord on the D string in order to place the 9th.

A♭/G♯ M7#11 *(Maj7#11, △#11)*

Root = A♭; maj 3rd = C; maj 7th = G; 11# = D

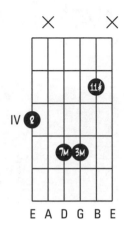

To play this type of M7#11 chord on the guitar, we have removed the 5th from the M7 chord on the B string in order to place the 11th#.

A♭/G♯ 7#11

Root = A♭; maj 3rd = C; min 7th = G♭; 11th# = D

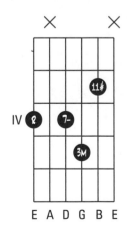

To play this type of 7#11 chord on the guitar, we have removed the 5th from the 7th chord on the B string in order to place the 11th#.

A♭/G♯ min7¹¹ (m7¹¹, -7¹¹)

Root = A♭; min 3rd = C♭ (B); min 7th = G♭; 11th = D♭

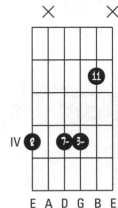

To play this type of min7¹¹ chord on the guitar, we have removed the 5th from the min7 chord on the B string, in order to place the perfect 11th.

A♭/G♯ M7 13 *(Maj7 13, △ 13)*

Root = A♭; maj 3rd = C; maj 7th = G; maj 13th = F

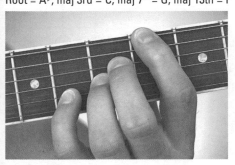

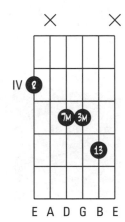

To play this type of M7 13 chord on the guitar, we have removed the 5th from the M7 chord on the B string, in order to place the major 13th.

A♭/G♯ 7¹³

Root = A♭; maj 3rd = C; min 7th = G♭; maj 13th = F

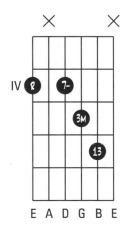

To play this type of 7¹³ chord on the guitar, we have removed the 5th from the 7th chord on the B string, in order to place the major 13th.

A♭/G♯ 7♭13

Root = A♭; maj 3rd = C; min 7th = G♭; 13th ♭ (min) = F♭ (E)

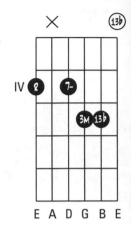

E A D G B E

To play this type of 7♭13 chord on the guitar, we have removed the 5th from the 7th chord on the B string, in order to place the minor 13th (13th♭).

Part X
A-family Chords

Amaj (M) *

Root = A; maj 3rd = C#; 5th = E

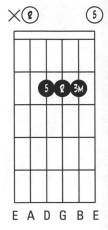

Amaj (M) *

Root = A; maj 3rd = C#; 5th = E

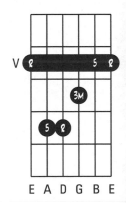

Amin (m, -)*

Root = A; min 3rd = C; 5th = E

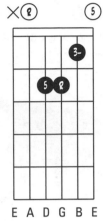

E A D G B E

To obtain a minor chord, lower the major 3rd of the major chord by a semitone (1 fret space) so that it becomes minor.

Amin (m, -)*

Root = A; min 3rd = C; 5th = E

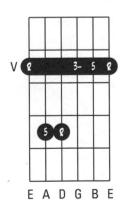

E A D G B E

To obtain a minor chord, lower the major 3rd of the major chord by a semitone (1 fret space) so that it becomes minor.

A6

Root = A; maj 3rd = C#; 5th = E; maj 6th = F#

For this type of 6th chord on the guitar, we have raised the 5th of the major chord on the high E string by a tone (2 fret spaces) so as to obtain the major 6th.

A6

Root = A; maj 3rd = C#; 5th = E; maj 6th = F#

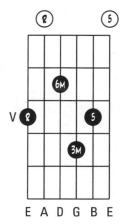

For this type of 6th chord on the guitar, we have lowered the root of the major chord on the D string by a tone and a half (3 fret spaces) so as to obtain the major 6th.

Amin6 *(m6, -6)*

Root = A; min 3rd = C; 5th = E; maj 6th = F#

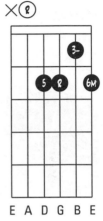

E A D G B E

For this type of min6th chord on the guitar, we have raised the 5th of the minor chord on the high E string by a tone (2 fret spaces) so as to obtain the major 6th.

Amin6 *(m6, -6)*

Root = A; min 3rd = C; 5th = E; maj 6th = F#

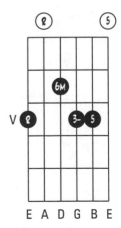

E A D G B E

For this type of min6th chord on the guitar, we have lowered the root minor chord on the D string by a tone and a half (3 fret spaces) so as to obtain the major 6th.

Asus4

Root = A; 4ᵗʰ = D; 5ᵗʰ = E

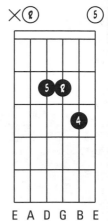

E A D G B E

To obtain a sus4 chord, raise the 3ʳᵈ of a major chord by a semitone (1 fret space) to that it becomes a 4ᵗʰ. A sus4 chord has no 3ʳᵈ: it is not major or minor.

Asus4

Root = A; 4ᵗʰ = D; 5ᵗʰ = E

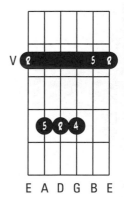

E A D G B E

If you find it hard to place this chord, you can omit the lowest 5ᵗʰ (on the A string), and find it of the B string.

A5 *

Root = A; 5th = E

×Ⓡ ×××

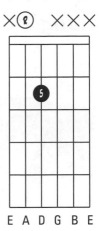

E A D G B E

These '5' chords only have 2 notes: the root and the 5th. Widely used in rock and heavy metal, they are also called *power chords*.

A5 *

Root = A; 5th = E

××××

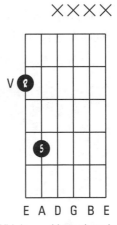

E A D G B E

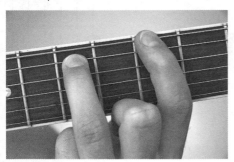

These '5' chords only have 2 notes: the root and the 5th. Widely used in rock and heavy metal, they are also called *power chords*.

280 Part X: A-family Chords

Aaug (#5, +, 5+)

Root = A; maj 3rd = C#; 5th# (aug) = E#(F)

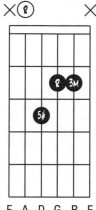

E A D G B E

An augmented chord is one in which the 5th is raised by a semitone (1 fret space).

Aaug (#5, +, 5+)

Root = A; maj 3rd = C#; 5th# (aug) = E#(F)

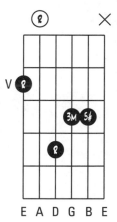

E A D G B E

If you find it hard to place this chord, you can just play the 3 highest notes of the chord. (The bass – in this case the root – can be omitted as it is repeated one octave above).

Adim (°)

Root = A; min 3rd = C; 5th$\flat$ (dim) = E$^\flat$

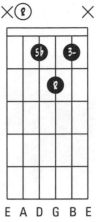

E A D G B E

A diminished chord is a major chord in which all the notes are lowered by a semitone (1 fret space), except for the root.

Adim (°)

Root = A; min 3rd = C; 5thb (dim) = E$^\flat$

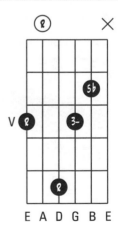

E A D G B E

If you find it hard to place this chord, you can just play the 3 highest notes of the chord. (The bass – in this case the root – can be omitted as it is repeated one octave above).

A^M7 (7M, Maj7, 7Maj, △)

Root = A; maj 3rd = C#; 5th = E; maj 7th = G#

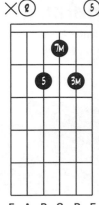

For this type of ^M7 chord on the guitar, we have lowered the root of the major chord on the G string by a semitone (1 fret space) to obtain the major 7th.

A^M7 (7M, Maj7, 7Maj, △)

Root = A; maj 3rd = C#; 5th = E; maj 7th = G#

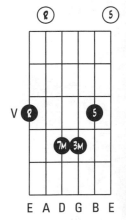

For this type of ^M7 chord on the guitar, we have lowered the root of the major chord on the D string by a semitone (1 fret space) to obtain the major 7th.

A7 *

Root = A; maj 3rd = C#; 5th = E; min 7th = G

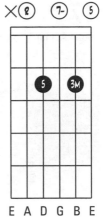

To obtain a 7 chord, lower the major 7th of the M7 chord by a semitone (1 fret space) so that it becomes minor.

A7 *

Root = A; maj 3rd = C#; 5th = E; min 7th = G

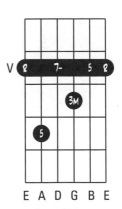

To obtain a 7 chord, lower the major 7th of the M7 chord by a semitone (1 fret space) so that it becomes minor.

A7 *

Root = A; maj 3rd = C#; 5th = E; min 7th = G

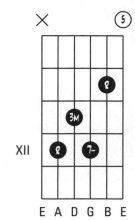

E A D G B E

For this type of 7 chord, which is widely used, we have removed the 5th from the major chord in order to place the minor 7th. Note that we can find the 5th on the high E string, played in the open position.

Amin7 (m7, -7)*

Root = A; min 3rd = C; 5th = E; min 7th = G

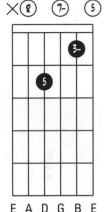

× ⑧ ⑦– ⑤

E A D G B E

To obtain a min 7 chord, lower the major 3rd of the 7 chord by a semitone (1 fret space) so that it becomes minor.

Amin7 (m7, -7)

Root = A; min 3rd = C; 5th = E; min 7th = G

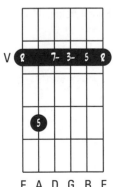

V ⑧ 7– 3– 5 ⑧

E A D G B E

To obtain a min 7 chord, lower the major 3rd of the 7 chord by a semitone (1 fret space) so that it becomes minor.

Amin7^{b5} (*m7^{b5}, -7^{b5}, ∅*)

Root = A; min 3rd = C; 5th^b (dim) = E^b; min 7th = G

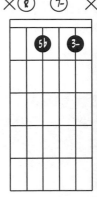

To obtain a min 7^{b5} chord, lower the 5th of the min7 chord by a semitone (1 fret space) so that it becomes a flattened 5th (also called a *diminished* 5th).

Amin7^{b5} (*m7^{b5}, -7^{b5}, ∅*)

Root = A; min 3rd = C; 5th^b (dim) = E^b; min 7th = G

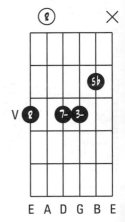

To obtain a min 7^{b5} chord, lower the 5th of the min7 chord by a semitone (1 fret space) so that it becomes a flattened 5th (also called a *diminished* 5th).

A7sus4

Root = A; 4th = D; 5th = E; min 7th = G

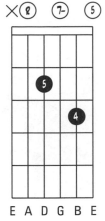

E A D G B E

To obtain a 7 sus4 chord, raise the major 3rd of the 7 chord by a semitone (1 fret space) so that it becomes the 4th. A 7 sus4 chord has no 3rd: it is not major or minor.

A7sus4

Root = A; 4th = D; 5th = E; min 7th = G

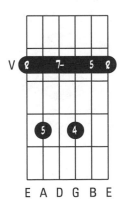

E A D G B E

TIP

If you find it hard to place this chord, you can omit the lowest 5th (on the A string), as you can find it on the B string.

Aaug7 (7#5, +7)

Root = A; maj 3rd = C#; 5th#(aug) = E#(F); min 7th = G

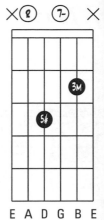

An aug7 chord is a 7 chord in which the 5th is raised by a semitone (1 fret space).

Aaug7 (7#5, +7)

Root = A; maj 3rd = C#; 5th#(aug) = E#(F); min 7th = G

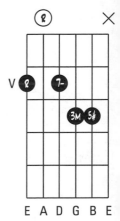

An aug7 chord is a 7 chord in which the 5th is raised by a semitone (1 fret space).

Adim 7 *(°7)*

Root = A; min 3rd = C; 5th♭ = E♭; dim 7th = G♭

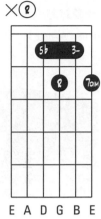

A dim 7 chord is a 7 chord in which all the notes are lowered by a semitone (1 fret space) except for the root.

Adim 7 *(°7)*

Root = A; min 3rd = C; 5th♭ = E♭; dim 7th = G♭

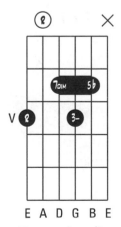

A dim 7 chord is a 7 chord in which all the notes are lowered by a semitone (1 fret space) except for the root.

Amin^{M7} *(-M7, min△, -△)*

Root = A; min 3rd = C; 5th = E; maj 7th = G#

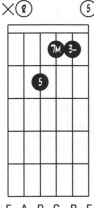

E A D G B E

To obtain a min^{M7} chord, raise the minor 7th of the min7 chord by a semitone (1 fret space), so that it becomes major.

Amin^{M7} *(-M7, min△, -△)*

Root = A; min 3rd = C; 5th = E; maj 7th = G#

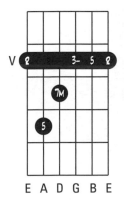

E A D G B E

To obtain a min^{M7} chord, raise the minor 7th of the min7 chord by a semitone (1 fret space), so that it becomes major.

Asus9

Root = A; 5th = E; 9th = B

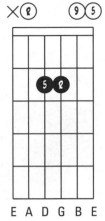

E A D G B E

To obtain a sus9 chord, lower the major 3rd of the major chord by a tone (2 fret spaces) so that it becomes the 9th. A sus9 chord has no 3rd: it is not major or minor.

Aadd9

Root = A; maj 3rd = C#; 5th = E; 9th = B

VII

E A D G B E

An add9 chord is a major chord with an added 9th.

$A^{M7\ 9}$ (Maj7, Δ9)

Root = A; maj 3rd = C#; maj 7th = G#; 9th = B

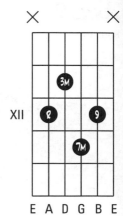

To play this type of $^{M7\ 9}$ chord on the guitar, we have removed the 5th from the ^{M7} chord on the D string in order to place the 9th.

$A7^9$

Root = A; maj 3rd = C#; min 7th = G; 9th = B

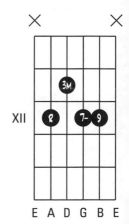

To play this type of 7^9 chord on the guitar, we have removed the 5th from the 7 chord on the D string in order to place the 9th.

$A^{7\flat9}$

Root = A; maj 3rd = C$^\sharp$; min 7th = G; 9$^{th\flat}$ = B$^\flat$

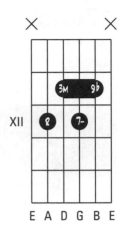

To play this type of 7$^{\flat9}$ chord on the guitar, we have removed the 5th from the 7 chord on the D string in order to place the 9$^{th\flat}$

$A7^{\sharp9}$

Root = A; maj 3rd = C$^\sharp$; min 7th = G; 9$^{th\sharp}$ = B$^\sharp$(C)

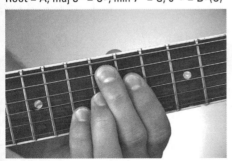

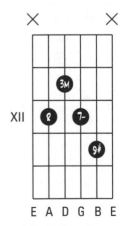

To play this type of 7$^{\sharp9}$ chord on the guitar, we have removed the 5th from the 7 chord on the D string in order to place the 9$^{th\sharp}$.

A7sus4⁹

Root = A; 4th = D; 5th = E; min 7th = G; 9th = B

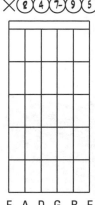

This type of 7 sus4⁹ is surely the easiest chord to play on the guitar because it consists solely of open chords! In a sus4⁹ chord, the 4th replaces the 3rd, so this chord is not major or minor.

Amin7⁹ (m7⁹, -7⁹)

Root = A; min 3rd = C; min 7th = G; 9th = B

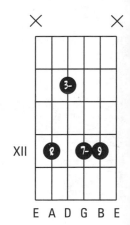

To play this type of min 7⁹ chord on the guitar, we have removed the 5th from the min7 chord on the D string so as to place the 9th.

$A^{M7\sharp11}$ *(Maj7#11, △11)*

Root = A; maj 3rd = C$\sharp$; maj 7th = G$\sharp$; 11$^{th}\sharp$ = D$\sharp$

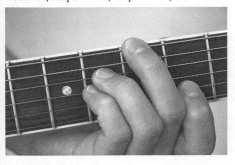
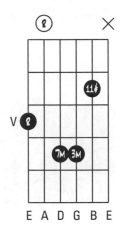

E A D G B E

To play this type of $^{M7}\sharp11$ chord on the guitar, we have removed the 5th from the ^{M7} chord on the B string so as to place the 11$^{th}\sharp$.

$A7\sharp11$

Root = A; maj 3rd = C$\sharp$; min 7th = G; 11$^{th}\sharp$ = D$\sharp$

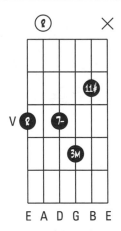

E A D G B E

To play this type of $^{7}\sharp11$ chord on the guitar, we have removed the 5th from the 7 chord on the B string so as to place the 11$^{th}\sharp$.

Amin7¹¹ (*m7¹¹*, *-7¹¹*)

Root = A; min 3rd = C; min 7th = G; 11th = D

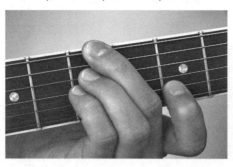

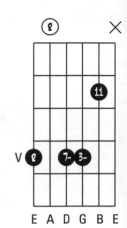

E A D G B E

To play this type of min7¹¹ chord on the guitar, we have removed the 5th from the min7 chord on the B string so as to place the perfect 11th .

$A^{M7\ 13}$ *(Maj7 13, △ 13)*

Root = A; maj 3rd = C#; maj 7th = G#; maj 13th = F#

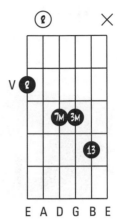

E A D G B E

To play this type of $^{M7\ 13}$ chord on the guitar, we have removed the 5th from the ^{M7} chord on the B string so as to place the major 13th.

$A7^{\ 13}$

Root = A; maj 3rd = C#; min 7th = G; maj 13th = F#

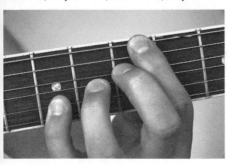

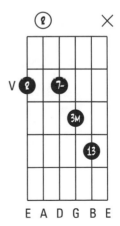

E A D G B E

To play this type of 7^{13} chord on the guitar, we have removed the 5th from the 7 chord on the B string so as to place the major 13th.

A7$^{\flat 13}$

Root = A; maj 3rd = C$\sharp$; min 7th = G; 13$^{th\,\flat(min)}$ = F

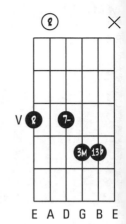

E A D G B E

To play this type of 7$^{\flat 13}$ chord on the guitar, we have removed the 5th from the 7 chord on the B string so as to place the minor 13th.

Part XI
B♭/A♯-family Chords

B♭/A♯ maj (M)*

Root = B♭; maj 3rd = D; 5th = F

×

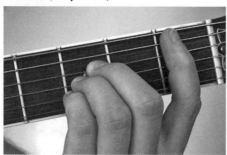

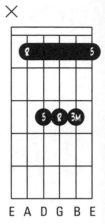

E A D G B E

B♭/A♯ maj (M)*

Root = B♭; maj 3rd = D; 5th = F

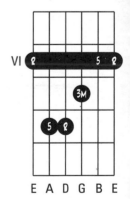

VI

E A D G B E

B♭/A♯ *min (m, -)*

Root = B♭; min 3rd = Db; 5th = F

To obtain a minor chord, lower the major 3rd of the major chord by a semitone (1 fret space) so that it becomes minor.

B♭/A♯ *min (m, -)*

Root = B♭; min 3rd = Db; 5th = F

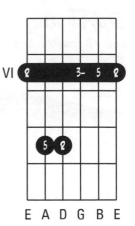

To obtain a minor chord, lower the major 3rd of the major chord by a semitone (1 fret space) so that it becomes minor.

B♭/A♯ 6

Root = B♭; maj 3rd = D; 5th = F; maj 6th = G

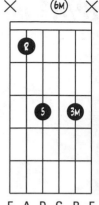

E A D G B E

For this type of 6 chord on the guitar, we have lowered the root of the major chord on the G string by a tone and a half (3 fret spaces) so as to obtain the major 6th.

B♭/A♯ 6

Root = B♭; maj 3rd = D; 5th = F; maj 6th = G

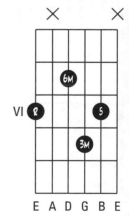

E A D G B E

For this type of 6 chord on the guitar, we have lowered the root of the major chord on the D string by a tone and a half (3 fret spaces) so as to obtain the major 6th.

B♭/A♯ *min6* (m6, -6)

Root = B♭; min 3rd = D♭; 5th = F; maj 6th = G

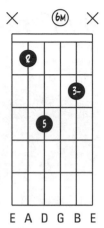

E A D G B E

For this type of min6 chord on the guitar, we have lowered the root of the minor chord on the G string by a tone and a half (3 fret spaces) so as to obtain the major 6th.

B♭/A♯ *min6* (m6, -6)

Root = B♭; min 3rd = D♭; 5th = F; maj 6th = G

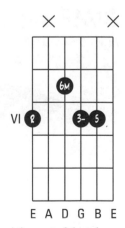

E A D G B E

For this type of min6 chord on the guitar, we have lowered the root of the minor chord on the D string by a tone and a half (3 fret spaces) so as to obtain the major 6th.

B♭/A♯ sus4

Root = B♭; 4th = E♭; 5th = F

×

E A D G B E

To obtain a sus4 chord, raise the 3rd of a major chord by a semitone (1 fret space) so that it becomes the 4th. A sus4 chord does not have a 3rd: it is not major or minor.

B♭/A♯ sus4

Root = B♭; 4th = E♭; 5th = F

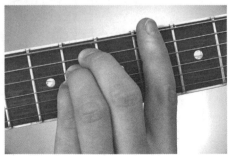

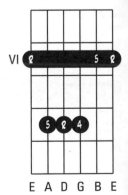

VI

E A D G B E

If you find it hard to place this chord, you can omit the lowest 5th (on the A string), and find it on the B string.

B♭/A# 5 *

Root = B♭; 5th = F

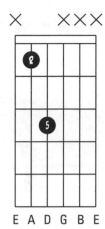

'5' chords only have 2 notes: the root and the 5th. Widely used in rock and heavy metal, they are also called *power chords*.

B♭/A# 5 *

Root = B♭; 5th = F

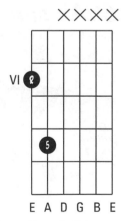

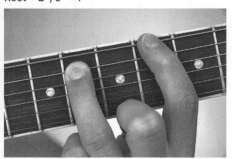

'5' chords only have 2 notes: the root and the 5th. Widely used in rock and heavy metal, they are also called *power chords*.

B♭/A# aug (#5, +, 5+)

Root = B♭; maj 3rd = D; 5th# = F#

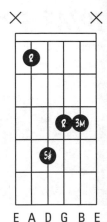

E A D G B E

An augmented chord is a major chord in which the 5th is raised a semitone (1 fret space).

B♭/A# aug (#5, +, 5+)

Root = B♭; maj 3rd = D; 5th# = F#

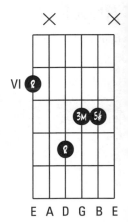

E A D G B E

If you find it hard to place this chord, you can just play the 3 highest notes of the chord. (The bass – in this case the root – can be omitted as it is repeated one octave above).

B♭/A♯ *dim* (°)

Root = B♭; min 3rd = Db; 5th♭ = F♭ (E)

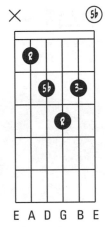

A diminished chord is a major chord in which all the notes are lowered a semitone (1 fret space), except for the root.

B♭/A♯ *dim* (°)

Root = B♭; min 3rd = D♭; 5th♭ = F♭ (E)

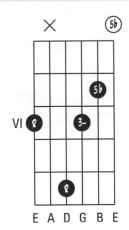

If you find it hard to place this chord, you can just play the 3 highest notes of the chord. (The bass – in this case the root – can be omitted as it is repeated one octave above).

B♭/A# M7 *(7M, Maj7, 7maj, △)*

Root = B♭; maj 3rd = D; 5th = F; maj 7th = A

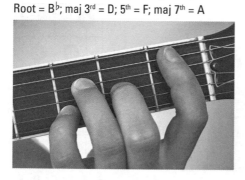

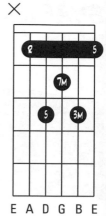

E A D G B E

For this type of M7 chord on the guitar, we have lowered the root of the major chord on the G string by a semitone (1 fret space) to obtain the major 7th.

B♭/A# M7 *(7M, Maj7, 7maj, △)*

Root = B♭; maj 3rd = D; 5th = F; maj 7th = A

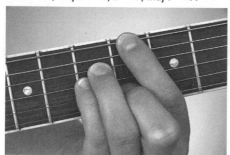

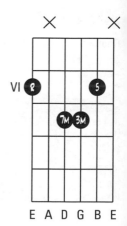

E A D G B E

For this type of M7 chord on the guitar, we have lowered the root of the major chord on the D string by a semitone (1 fret space) to obtain the major 7th.

B♭/A♯ 7

Root = B♭; maj 3rd = D; 5th = F; min 7th = A♭

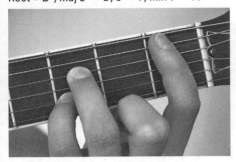

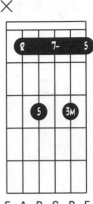

To obtain a 7 chord, lower the major 7th of the ^{M7} chord by a semitone (1 fret space) so that it becomes minor.

B♭/A♯ 7

Root = B♭; maj 3rd = D; 5th = F; min 7th = A♭

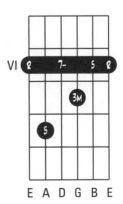

To obtain a 7 chord, lower the major 7th of the ^{M7} chord by a semitone (1 fret space) so that it becomes minor.

B♭/A♯ 7 *

Root = B♭; maj 3rd = D; min 7th = A♭

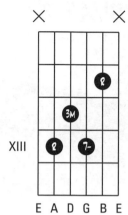

Note that for this type of 7 chord, which is widely used, we have removed the 5th of the major chord in order to place the minor 7th.

B♭/A♯ min7 (m7, -7)

Root = B♭; min 3rd = D♭; 5th = F; min 7th = A♭

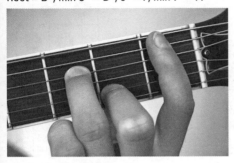

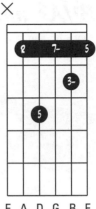

To obtain a min7 chord, lower the major 3rd of the 7 chord by a semitone (1 fret space) so that it becomes minor.

B♭/A♯ min7 (m7, -7)

Root = B♭; min 3rd = D♭; 5th = F; min 7th = A♭

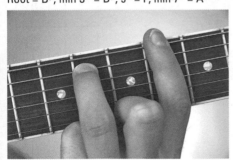

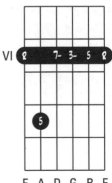

To obtain a min7 chord, lower the major 3rd of the 7 chord by a semitone (1 fret space) so that it becomes minor.

B♭/A♯ *min 7♭5* (m7♭5, -7♭5, ∅)

× ⑤♭

Root = B♭; min 3ʳᵈ = D♭; 5th♭ = Fb(E); min 7ᵗʰ = A♭

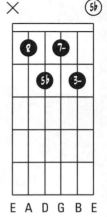

E A D G B E

To obtain a min7♭5 chord, lower the 5ᵗʰ of the min7 chord by a semitone (1 fret space), so that it becomes a flattened 5ᵗʰ (also called a *diminished 5th*).

B♭/A♯ *min 7♭5* (m7♭5, -7♭5, ∅)

× ⑤♭

Root = B♭; min 3ʳᵈ = D♭; 5th♭ = F♭ (E); min 7ᵗʰ = A♭

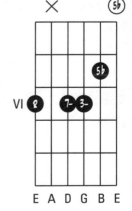

E A D G B E

To obtain a min7♭5 chord, lower the 5ᵗʰ of the min7 chord by a semitone (1 fret space), so that it becomes a flattened 5ᵗʰ (also called a *diminished 5th*).

B♭/A♯ 7sus4

Root = B♭; 4th = E♭; 5th = F; min 7th = A♭

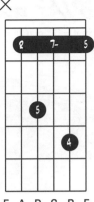

E A D G B E

To obtain a 7sus4 chord, raise the major 3rd of the 7 chord by a semitone (1 fret space) so that it becomes the 4th. A 7sus4 chord does not have a 3rd: it is not major or minor.

B♭/A♯ 7sus4

Root = B♭; 4th = E♭; 5th = F; min 7th = A♭

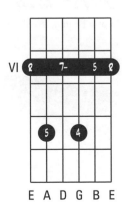

E A D G B E

TIP

If you find it hard to place this chord, you can omit the lowest 5th (on the A string), as it can be found on the B string.

B♭/A♯ aug7 (7♯5, +7)

Root = B♭; maj 3rd = D; 5th = F♯; min 7th = A♭

An aug7 chord is a 7 chord in which the 5th is raised by a semitone (1 box). Note that even if you press on the high E string because of the barre, you should not play it.

B♭/A♯ aug7 (7♯5, +7)

Root = B♭; maj 3rd = D; 5th = F♯; min 7th = A♭

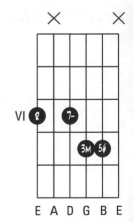

An aug7 chord is a 7 chord in which the 5th is raised by a semitone (1 fret space).

B♭/A# *dim7* (°7)

Root = B♭; min 3rd = D♭; 5th♭ = F♭ (E); dim7th = Abb(G)

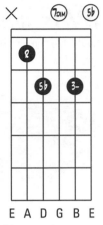

A dim7 chord is a 7 chord in which all the notes are lowered by a semitone (1 fret space), except for the root.

B♭/A# *dim7* (°7)

Root = B♭; min 3rd = D♭; 5th♭ = F♭ (E); dim7th = A♭♭ (G)

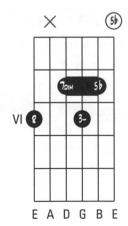

A dim7 chord is a 7 chord in which all the notes are lowered by a semitone (1 fret space), except for the root.

B♭/A# min^M7 (-^M7, min^Δ, -^Δ)

Root = B♭; min 3rd = D♭; 5th = F; maj 7th = A

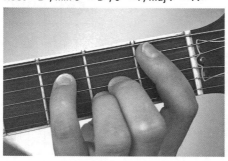

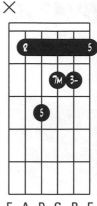

To obtain a min^M7 chord, raise the minor 7th of the min7 chord by a semitone (1 fret space) so that it becomes major.

B♭/A# min^M7 (-^M7, min^Δ, -^Δ)

Root = B♭; min 3rd = D♭; 5th = F; maj 7th = A

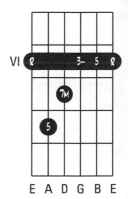

To obtain a min^M7 chord, raise the minor 7th of the min7 chord by a semitone (1 fret space) so that it becomes major.

B♭/A♯ sus9

Root = B♭; 5th = F; 9th = C

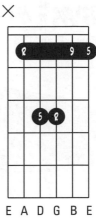

To obtain a sus9 chord, lower the major 3rd of the major chord by a tone (2 fret spaces) so that it becomes the 9th. A sus9 chord has no 3rd: it is not major or minor.

B♭/A♯ add9

Root = B♭; maj 3rd = D; 5th = F; 9th = C

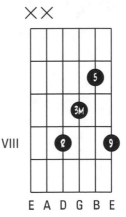

An add9 chord is a major chord with an added 9th.

B♭/A♯ M7 9 *(Maj7 9, △9)*

Root = B♭; maj3rd = D; maj7th = A; 9th = C

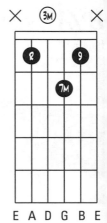

E A D G B E

To play this type of M7 9 chord on the guitar, we have removed the 5th from the M7 chord on the D string so as to place the 9th.

B♭/A♯ 7⁹

Root = B♭; maj 3rd = D; min 7th = A; 9th = C

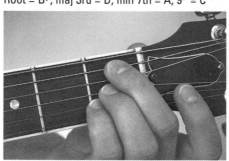

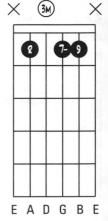

E A D G B E

To play this type of 7⁹ chord on the guitar, we have removed the 5th from the 7 chord on the D string so as to place the 9th.

B♭/A# 7♭9

Root = B♭; maj 3rd = D; min7th = A♭; 9thb = C♭ (B)

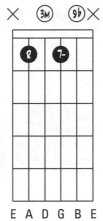

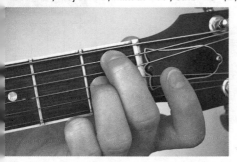

To play this type of 7♭9 chord on the guitar, we have removed the 5th from the 7 chord on the D string so as to place the 9thb.

B♭/A# 7#9

Root = B♭; maj 3rd = D; min7th = Ab; 9th# = C#

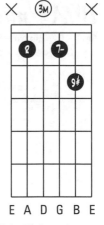

To play this type of 7#9 chord on the guitar, we have removed the 5th from the 7 chord on the D string so as to place the 9th#.

B♭/A♯ 7sus4⁹

Root = B♭; 4th = Eb; 5th = F; min7th = A♭; 9th = C

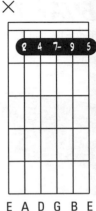

To obtain a 7sus4⁹ chord, raise the major 3rd of the 7⁹ chord by a semitone (1 fret space) so that it becomes the 4th. A 7sus4⁹ chord has no 3rd: it is not major or minor.

B♭/A♯ min7⁹ (m7⁹, -7⁹)

Root – B♭; min3rd = D♭; min7th = A♭; 9th = C

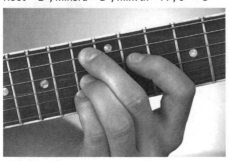

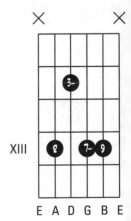

E A D G B E

To play this type of min7⁹ chord on the guitar, we have removed the 5th from the min7 chord on the D string, so as to place the 9th.

$B♭/A♯$ M7 ♯ 11 *(Maj 7♯11, △♯11)*

Root = B♭; maj 3rd = D; maj 7th = A; 11th♯ = E

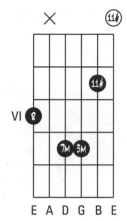

To play this type of M7♯11 chord on the guitar, we have removed the 5th from the M7 chord on the B string, so as to place the 11th♯.

$B♭/A♯$ 7♯11

Root = B♭; maj 3rd = D; min7th = A♭; 11th♯ = E

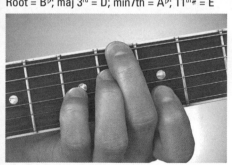

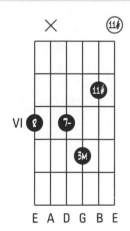

To play this type of 7♯11 chord on the guitar, we have removed the 5th from the 7 chord on the B string, so as to place the 11th♯.

B♭/A# min7¹¹ (m7¹¹, -7¹¹)

Root = B♭; min3rd = D♭; min7th = A♭; 11th = E♭

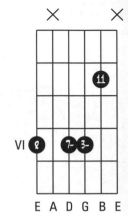

To play this type of min7¹¹ chord on the guitar, we have removed the 5th from the min7 chord on the B string to as to place the perfect 11th.

B♭/A♯ M7 13 *(Maj7 13, △13)*

Root = B♭; maj 3rd = D; maj 7th = A; maj 13th = G

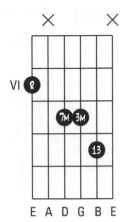

To play this type of M7 13 chord on the guitar, we have removed the 5th from the M7 chord on the B string to as to place the major 13th.

B♭/A♯ 7¹³

Root = B♭; maj 3rd = D; min7th = A♭; maj 13th = G

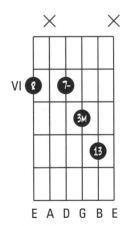

To play this type of 7¹³ chord on the guitar, we have removed the 5th from the 7 chord on the B string to as to place the major 13th.

B♭/A# 7♭ 13

Root = B♭; maj 3rd = D; min 7th = A♭; 13th♭ (min) = G♭

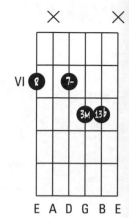

VI

7-

3M 13♭

E A D G B E

To play this type of 7♭13 chord on the guitar, we have removed the 5th from the 7 chord on the B string to as to place the minor 13th (13♭).

Part XII
B-family Chords

Bmaj (m)*

Root = B; maj 3 = D#; 5th = F#

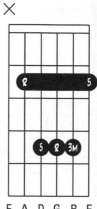

E A D G B E

Bmaj (m)*

Root = B; maj 3 = D#; 5th = F#

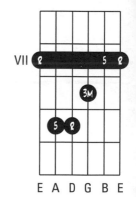

E A D G B E

Bmin *(m, -)**

Root = B; min 3rd = D; 5th = F#

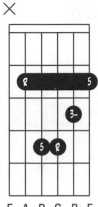

To obtain a minor chord, lower the major 3rd of the major chord by a semitone (1 fret space) so that it becomes minor.

Bmin *(m, -)**

Root = B; min 3rd = D; 5th = F#

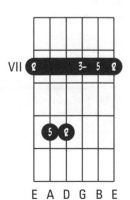

To obtain a minor chord, lower the major 3rd of the major chord by a semitone (1 fret space) so that it becomes minor.

B6

Root = B; maj 3rd = D$^\sharp$; maj 6th = G$^\sharp$

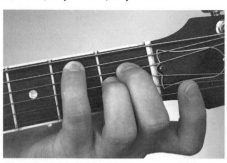

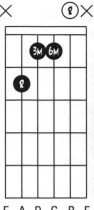

To play this type of chord on the guitar, we have removed the 5th from the major chord so as to place the major 6th.

B6

Root = B; maj 3rd = D$^\sharp$; 5th = F$^\sharp$; maj 6th = G$^\sharp$

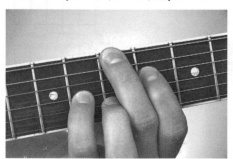

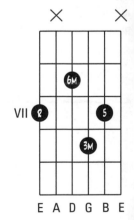

For this type of chord on the guitar, we have lowered the root of the major chord on the D string by a tone and a half (3 fret spaces) to obtain the major 6th.

Bmin6 *(m6, -6)*

Root = B; min 3rd = D; 5th = F#; maj 6th = G#

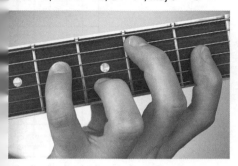

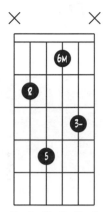

For this type of min6 chord on the guitar, we have lowered the root of the minor chord on the G string by a tone and a half (3 fret spaces) to obtain the major 6th.

E A D G B E

Bmin6 *(m6, -6)*

Root = B; min 3rd = D; 5th = F#; maj 6th = G#

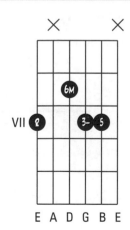

VII

E A D G B E

For this type of min6 chord on the guitar, we have lowered the root of the minor chord on the D string by a tone and a half (3 fret spaces) to obtain the major 6th.

Bsus4

Root = B; 4th = E; 5th = F♯

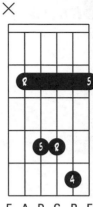

E A D G B E

To obtain a sus4 chord, raise the 3rd of a major chord by a semitone (1 fret space) so that it becomes the 4th. A sus 4 chord has no 3rd: it is not major or minor.

Bsus4

Root = B; 4th = E; 5th = F♯

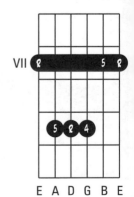

E A D G B E

If you find it hard to place this chord, you can omit the lowest 5th (on the A string), and find it on the B string.

B5*

Root = B; 5th = F#

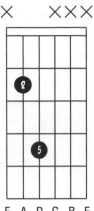

'5' chords only have 2 notes: the root and the 5th. Widely used in rock and heavy metal, they are also called *power chords*.

B5*

Root = B; 5th = F#

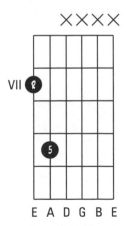

'5' chords only have 2 notes: the root and the 5th. Widely used in rock and heavy metal, they are also called *power chords*.

Baug (#5, 5+)

Root = B; maj 3rd = D#; 5th# = F##(G)

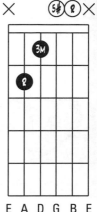

An augmented chord is a major chord in which the 5th is raised by a semitone (1 fret space).

Baug (#5, 5+)

Root = B; maj 3rd = D#; 5th# = F##(G)

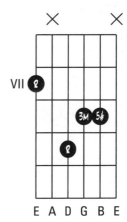

E A D G B E

If you find it hard to place this chord, you can just play the 3 highest notes of the chord. (The bass – in this case the root – can be omitted as it is repeated one octave above.)

Bdim (°)

Root = B; min3rd = D; 5th♭ = F

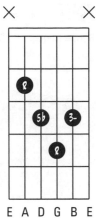

E A D G B E

A diminished chord is a major chord in which all the notes are lowered by a semitone (1 fret space) except for the root.

Bdim (°)

Root = B; min3rd = D; 5th♭ = F

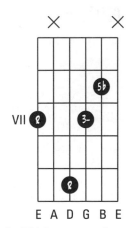

E A D G B E

If you find it hard to place this chord, you can just play the 3 highest notes of the chord. (The bass – in this case the root – can be omitted as it is repeated one octave above).

B^{M7} *(7M, maj7, 7maj, △)*

Root = B; maj3rd = D#; 5th = F#; maj7th = A#

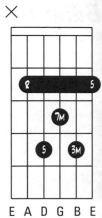

For this type of ^{M7} chord on the guitar, we have lowered the root of the major chord on the G string by a semitone (1 fret space) to obtain the major 7th.

B^{M7} *(7M, maj7, 7maj, △)*

Root = B; maj3rd = D#; 5th = F#; maj7th = A#

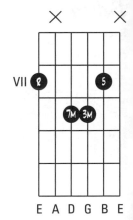

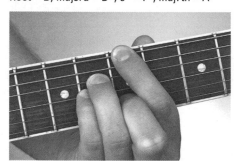

For this type of ^{M7} chord on the guitar, we have lowered the root of the major chord on the D string by a semitone (1 fret space) to obtain the major 7th.

B7 *

Root = B; maj3rd = D$\sharp$; 5th = F$\sharp$; min7th = A

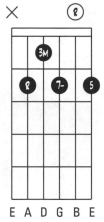

E A D G B E

---

*B7**

Root = B; maj3rd = D$\sharp$; 5th = F$\sharp$; min7th = A

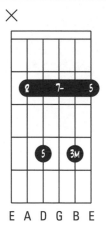

E A D G B E

To obtain a 7 chord, lower the major 7th of the M7 chord by a semitone (1 fret space) so that it becomes minor.

B7

Root = B; maj3rd = D$^\sharp$; 5th = F$^\sharp$; min7th = A

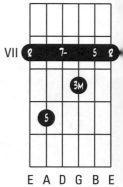

E A D G B E

To obtain a 7 chord, lower the major 7th of the ^{M7} chord by a semitone (1 fret space) so that it becomes minor.

Bmin7 (m7, -7)

Root = B; min3rd = D; 5ᵗʰ = F♯; min7th = A

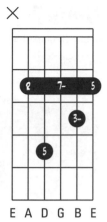

To obtain a min7 chord, lower the major 3ʳᵈ of the 7 chord by a semitone (1 fret space) so that it becomes minor.

Bmin7 (m7, -7)

Root = B; min3rd = D; 5ᵗʰ = F♯; min7th = A

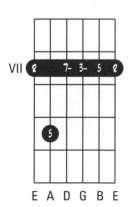

To obtain a min7 chord, lower the major 3ʳᵈ of the 7 chord by a semitone (1 fret space) so that it becomes minor.

$Bmin7^{b5}$ ($m7^{b5}$, -7^{b5}, $ø$)

Root = B; min3rd = D; 5th^b = F; min7th = A

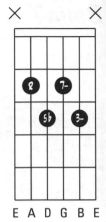

To obtain a min7^{b5} chord, lower the 5th of the min7 chord by a semitone, so that it becomes a flattened 5th (also called a *diminished 5th*).

$Bmin7^{b5}$ ($m7^{b5}$, -7^{b5}, $ø$)

Root = B; min3rd = D; 5th^b = F; min7th = A

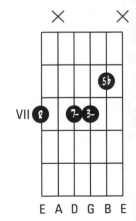

To obtain a min7^{b5} chord, lower the 5th of the min7 chord by a semitone, so that it becomes a flattened 5th (also called a *diminished 5th*).

B7sus4

Root = B; 4th = E; 5th = F#; min7th = A

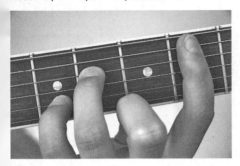

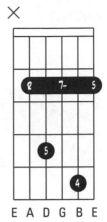

To obtain a 7sus4 chord, raise the major 3rd of the 7 chord by a semitone (1 fret space) to that it becomes the 4th. A 7sus4 chord has no 3rd: it is not major or minor.

B7sus4

Root = B; 4th = E; 5th = F#; min7th = A

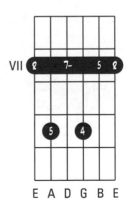

If you find it hard to place this chord, you can omit the lowest 5th (on the A string), and find it on the B string.

Baug7 (7♯5, +7)

Root = B; maj 3rd = D♯; 5th♯ = F♯♯(G); min 7th = A

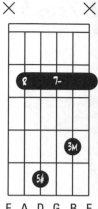

An aug7 chord is a 7 chord in which the 5th is raised by a semitone (1 fret space). Note that even if you press on the high E chord because of the barre, you should not play it.

Baug7 (7♯5, +7)

Root = B; maj 3rd = D♯; 5th♯ = F♯♯(G); min 7th = A

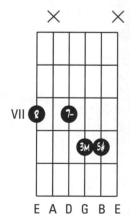

An aug7 chord is a 7 chord in which the 5th is raised by a semitone (1 fret space).

Bdim7 *(°7)*

Root = B; min3rd = D; 5th♭ = F; dim 7th = Ab

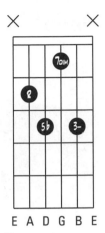

E A D G B E

A dim7 chord is a 7 chord in which all the notes are lowered by a semitone (1 fret space), except for the root.

Bdim7 *(°7)*

Root = B; min3rd = D; 5th♭ = F; dim 7th = A♭

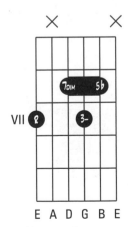

E A D G B E

A dim7 chord is a 7 chord in which all the notes are lowered by a semitone (1 fret space), except for the root.

$Bmin^{M7}$ (-M7, min△, -△)

Root = B; min 3rd = D = 5th = F#; maj 7th = A#

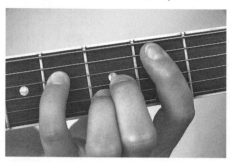

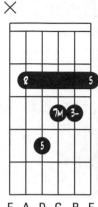

E A D G B E

To obtain a min^{M7} chord, raise the minor 7th of the min7 chord by a semitone (1 fret space) so that it becomes major.

$Bmin^{M7}$ (-M7, min△, -△)

Root = B; min 3rd = D = 5th = F#; maj 7th = A#

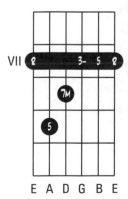

VII

E A D G B E

To obtain a min^{M7} chord, raise the minor 7th of the min7 chord by a semitone (1 fret space) so that it becomes major.

Bsus9

Root = B; 5th = F#; 9th = C#

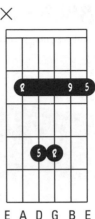

To obtain a sus9 chord, lower the major 3rd of the major chord by a tone (2 fret spaces) so that it becomes the 9th. A sus9 chord has no 3rd: it is not major or minor.

Badd9

Root = B; maj3rd = D#; 5th = F#; 9th = C#

An add9 chord is a major chord with an added 9th.

$B^{M7\ 9}$ (Maj7 9, Δ9)

Root = B; maj 3rd = D#; maj 7th = A#; 9th = C#

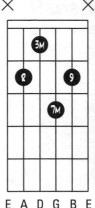

E A D G B E

To play this type of chord on the guitar, we have removed the 5th from the M7 chord on the D string so as to place the 9th.

$B7^9$

Root = B; maj 3rd = D#; min 7th = A; 9th = C#

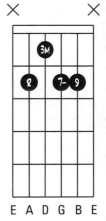

E A D G B E

To play this type of chord on the guitar, we have removed the 5th from the 7 chord on the D string so as to place the 9th.

$B7^{b9}$

Root = B; maj 3rd = D#; min 7th = A; 9^{thb} = C

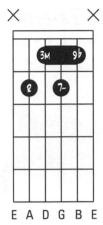

E A D G B E

To play this type of 7^{b9} chord on the guitar, we have removed the 5th from the 7 chord on the D string so as to place the 9^{thb}.

$B7^{\sharp 9}$

Root = B; maj 3rd = D#; min 7th = A; $9^{th\sharp}$ = C##(D)

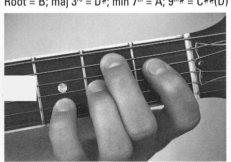

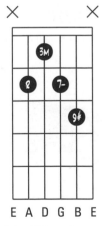

E A D G B E

To play this type of $7^{\sharp}9$ chord on the guitar, we have removed the 5th from the 7 chord on the D string so as to place the 9th.

B7sus4⁹

Root = B; 4ᵗʰ = E; 5ᵗʰ = F♯; min 7ᵗʰ = C♯

To obtain a 7sus4⁹ chord, raise the major 3ʳᵈ of the 7⁹ chord by a semitone (1 fret space) to that it becomes the 4ᵗʰ. A 7sus4⁹ chord has no 3ʳᵈ: it is not major or minor.

Bmin7⁹ (m7⁹, -7⁹)

Root = B; min 3ʳᵈ = D; min 7ᵗʰ = A; 9ᵗʰ = C♯

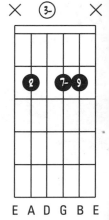

To play this type of min7⁹ chord on the guitar, we have removed the 5ᵗʰ from the min7 chord on the D string so as to place the 9ᵗʰ.

B^{M7} ♯ 11 _(Maj7♯11, △♯11)_

Root = B; maj 3rd = D♯; maj 7th = A♯; 11th♯ = E♯(F)

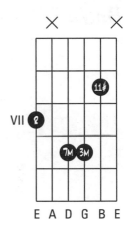

To play this type of ^{M7}♯^{11} chord on the guitar, we have removed the 5th from the ^{M7} chord on the B string so as to place the 11th♯.

$B7$ ♯ 11

Root = B; maj 3rd = D♯; min 7th = A; 11th♯ = E♯(F)

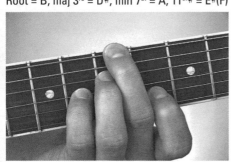

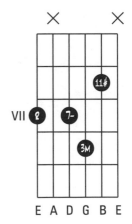

To play this type of 7♯^{11} chord on the guitar, we have removed the 5th from the 7 chord on the B string so as to place the 11th♯.

Bmin7 ^{11} *(m7*^{11}*, -7*^{11}*)*

Root = B; min 3rd = D; min 7th = A; 11th = E

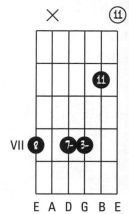

E A D G B E

To play this type of min7^{11} chord on the guitar, we have removed the 5th from the min7 chord on the B string so as to place the perfect 11th.

$B^{M7\ 13}$ *(Maj7, Δ 13)*

Root = B; maj 3rd = D#; maj 7th = A#; maj 13th = G#

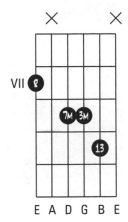

To play this type of ^{M7}#13 chord on the guitar, we have removed the 5th from the ^{M7} chord on the B string so as to place the major13th.

$B7^{13}$

Root = B; maj 3rd = D#; min 7th = A; maj 13th = G#

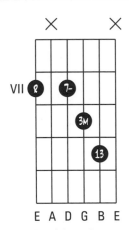

To play this type of 7^{13} chord on the guitar, we have removed the 5th from the 7 chord on the B string so as to place the major 13th.

$B7^{b\,13}$

Root = B; maj 3rd = D$^\sharp$; min 7th = A; 13^{thb}(min) = G

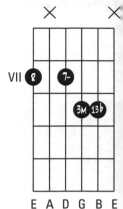

To play this type of 7^{b13} chord on the guitar, we have removed the 5th from the 7 chord on the B string so as to place the minor 13th (13^b).

Index

• A-family Chords •

• A#/B♭-family Chords •

• B-family Chords •

• C-family Chords •

• $C^{\#}/D^{b}$-family Chords •

• D-family Chords •

• D#/E♭-family Chords •

• E-family Chords •

• G-family Chords •

• G#/A♭-family Chords •

FOR DUMMIES

Making Everything Easier!™

UK editions

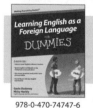

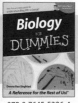
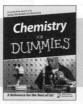

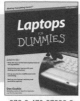

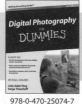
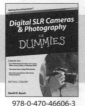